D0843329

# The Going

Leon Wiener Dow

# The Going

A Meditation on Jewish Law

Leon Wiener Dow
Shalom Hartman Institute
Jerusalem, Israel

ISBN 978-3-319-68830-5     ISBN 978-3-319-68831-2     (eBook)
https://doi.org/10.1007/978-3-319-68831-2

Library of Congress Control Number: 2017955227

Cover pattern © Melisa Hasan

Printed on acid-free paper

This Palgrave Macmillan imprint is published by Springer Nature
The registered company is Springer International Publishing AG
The registered company address is: Gewerbestrasse 11, 6330 Cham, Switzerland

*With unending appreciation and boundless love—*
*To those who tread before me, Mom and Dad;*
*she who walks beside me, Bruria;*
*and those who will continue along the way, Yael, Shiraz, Yifat, Yiska, and*
*Evyatar*

# Acknowledgments

This work began during a remarkable year that I spent at Berkeley Law as a postdoctoral fellow of the Berkeley Institute for Jewish Law and Israel Studies, and the Robbins Collection for Religious and Civil Law. The respite from my teaching duties in Israel allowed me to embark upon this project, one of a markedly different tenor from what I had done until then—and from what my colleagues at the Institute were doing. The support I received was unflagging, and the community of visiting scholars among whom I found myself was stimulating and nurturing. My heartfelt thanks to Daniella Beinisch, former Director of the Institute, and to Laurent Mayali, Director of the Robbins Collection. A special thanks to Kenneth Bamberger, Faculty Director of the Institute, for making the year possible, and, once a reality, for going well beyond what I could reasonably expect a colleague and friend to do.

My work on the project continued once I had returned to Jerusalem and found my new-old home at the Shalom Hartman Institute, where I serve as a research fellow. I am blessed at the Institute with colleagues who understand the exigency of allowing the voice of Torah to issue forth "today." A special thanks to President of the Institute, Donniel Hartman, for the remarkable ability to keep his line of vision raised to the horizon without, even momentarily, losing sight of the details on the ground.

Once I had a manuscript in hand, I trusted it to my dear friends and colleagues, Leon Morris and Benjamin Pollock. They were as readers as they are as people: generous and kind, insightful and probing, thoroughgoing and deep. I am profoundly grateful to them for their time, wisdom, and friendship.

Also at that early stage—and at every subsequent step along the way—I shared it with my beloved brother, Mark Dow. Mark's understanding of what I was after—and how I might get there, given both the limits and the potentialities of words, spoken and written—was astounding. He pored over the manuscript, keeping one keen, editorial, creative eye focused on the words, while the other glanced steadfastly at me. It is a manifest gift to have a kindred soul in one's life; it is arresting to have that person be my brother, whose steadfast support and love have been so significant for me, over the course of so many years.

My wise and devoted brother David Dow provided, along with Mark, key insights at critical junctions along the way of turning this from a manuscript into a book.

For helping me find references that I was looking for based on only the vaguest of recollections, I am indebted to my friends and colleagues: Adam Afterman, Mimi Feigelson, Daniel Price, Biti Roi, and Gila Vachman. A special thanks to Peretz Rodman for his help on the transliterations.

I was blessed to have Sam Mellins, a former student, serve as a research assistant as I prepared the book for production. Sam's diligence in preparing the index and in tracking down sources was rivaled only by the beyond-his-years wisdom of his editorial suggestions.

When the time came to find a publisher, I was not sanguine, given the unorthodox, hybrid nature of this work. I cannot imagine a more fortuitous event than to have found Phil Getz of Palgrave Macmillan, the book's editor. He understood the deeper aspiration of the project while remaining attentive to the possibilities and realities of the publication process. One of Phil's characteristically wise moves was to send it out for review to Ariel Evan Mayse, who—once the book had been accepted—renounced anonymity and generously offered me his time and wisdom to help improve the work. Ariel's fusion of rigorous scholarship and insistence upon the existential relevance of the material proved to be a perfect match, enabling an appreciative critique of the manuscript. Amy Invernizzi, Assistant Editor at Palgrave, provided crucial and responsive editorial help along the way.

And finally, there are those whose constancy in my life places them on every page of this book.

My ḥevruta, Joel Levy, is the person with whom I learned the vast majority of the texts herein. His wisdom, his voice, his laughter, his incisive critique: they are inseparable from my own learning, present for me even in his absence.

My parents, Melvin Dow and Frieda Katz Dow, have always been an unwavering source of love and support. They not only allowed me to tread my path, even when it diverged from theirs; they abetted me along my way, valuing it and trusting me. That was and remains not only a supreme source of nourishment for me, but also my highest aspiration as a parent. My parents-in-law, Menachem and Miriam Wiener, are my parents *in sito*, offering caring, affection, and unflagging support.

Bruria, my partner on this journey, is my supreme teacher in every crevice of my life. Aramaic for wife is דביתו [*de-veito*], "of his home," an ancient-world, gendered rendering of what a wife is. Bruria manages to invigorate this term with new possibility, establishing a home in the deepest sense of the word: she is a source of containment and placidity; a wellspring of constancy; a safe space to let my guard down and my ideas flow; and my grounding and orientation. With her, I have had the privilege of bringing five beautiful, independent souls into this world, shepherding them along their way. Yael, Shiraz, Yifat, Yiska, and Evyatar are our greatest source of joy and the touchstone of how well we are faring at establishing harmony between the Torah that we talk and the halakha that we live.

# CONTENTS

# LIST OF ABBREVIATIONS AND NOTE ON TEXTUAL REFERENCES AND TRANSLATIONS

The following abbreviations have been used in notes:

- B.T. = Babylonian Talmud, followed by the name of the tractate and folio.
- J.T. = Jerusalem Talmud, followed by the name of the tractate, chapter, and *halakha*.

References to traditional texts follow conventional format:

- Genesis 1:1 = Genesis Chapter 1, verse 1
- Mishna Berakhot 1:1 = Mishna Tracate Berakhot Chapter 1 Mishna 1

All translations are mine unless otherwise noted.

# Beginnings

**Abstract** This chapter offers an autobiographical accounting of Wiener Dow's journey to the halakha. From his childhood in Houston, Texas, in which he was drawn toward a Jewish praxis incommensurate with his surroundings, through his college years, and into his years studying for personal rabbinic ordination from Rabbi David Hartman, his path reveals an attentiveness to a commanding voice—and to a community that tries to give expression, though its rigorous praxis, to a life of devotion to the Divine.

This autobiographical starting point results not only from the author's philosophical commitments, but also from his understanding of halakha as a form of open-ended doing that requires a willingness to negotiate simultaneous commitments to personal authenticity, communal norm, and the command of the Divine.

**Keywords** halakha and authenticity • Jewish spiritual biography • halakha as personal journey • Leibowitz, Hartman, and Heschel

God is not first. The word precedes God. The Torah precedes God. The community precedes God. The world precedes God. The world precedes the family precedes the community precedes the Torah precedes God.

In the beginning is relation, writes Buber.[1] The nursing baby becomes a metaphor for all human experience: bobbing on her mother's breast until she finds the nipple, she latches on and begins to nurse, the milk she ingests a liquid expression of the flowing connection that occurs in all contact. The tiny fingers caress and mindlessly inch toward the torso, the first indication—not yet intelligible to the infant—that she is seeking and will discover a deeper connection: attached to this breast is an entire human being, her mother. The gaze lifts up, eventually meeting eyes. Over time, her eyes will respond, she will smile.

These moments envelop and reveal the deepest of life's recesses: intimacy; majesty; mystery; an intersubjectivity that weaves together seamlessly dependence and independence; the extension toward infinity from and through the sinews of this world.

Rosenzweig teaches us that we never actually separate the individual sinews out from the flesh in which they're embedded. True, we can remove them surgically for examination, but we only "know" them in their interrelatedness, in their movement.[2]

We understand this intuitively: we want someone to know us, so we invite them to our home, so that they meet our spouse, our children, our parents, our siblings: once they know us, once they know where we're from, once they've seen the bedroom from which we speak to them on the phone, once they've seen our neighborhood, once they've seen us play the guitar, once they've met our friends, once they've … *then* they will know us, truly know us, for they will have seen us in our elements, they will have seen us in our genuine, living relations.

Our journey—for what is this kind of exploration if not a journey that we share right now, at this very moment?—must then begin with those remembered beginnings, those relations and relationships, which lead me to where I am now, which oriented me and which pointed me toward the path on which I travel. Sometimes on the path, sometimes straying from it spontaneously; sometimes plodding ahead through a thicket, other times along a ledge from which I can gaze upon the splendor of the view.

It is always my path, but I would not write this were I not to believe that my path may well provide a point of orientation and reorientation for someone other than me. But I wish to make a stronger, less personal claim, one that I will substantiate later: the *halakha*, the Jewish being-on-the-way, is, fundamentally, a communal praxis. Like music, which is made not by the notes but by the intervals between them, as they are played over time—the halakha stakes its communal existence on our willingness and ability to seek points of convergence and divergence between our paths. And so my path, like the path of every individual who situates herself in the nexus of Jewish shared living, affects the whole truly, albeit diffusely, by affecting those whose travels take them in my proximity, whether they cross my path, journey along part of it at a different pace, or connect to it only through the "ecosystem" of paths and trails.

This chapter, then, is my attempt to retrace my own way to the halakha. The moment that beckons as a starting point finds me at the breakfast room table in my parents' home in Houston, Texas. I am 15, doing homework, my mother's comforting presence at the table, my brother Mark, 23 years old, preparing himself something to eat in the kitchen. Mark is visiting from New York City, where he is waiting on tables so that he can eke out a living and write poetry. Mark had graduated from an Ivy League school, and was thrusting himself head-first into a life that—even were he to be successful on his own terms—would put him grossly out of step with the measures of success amid which we grew.

"I really respect what you're doing with your life," I tell him.

"Thanks," he says. He pauses and then adds casually: "But I don't know what the hell I'm doing with my life."

I think that even then I understood the depth contained in that moment. In part, I was witness to the chasm that separates how we appear from the outside and how we experience ourselves on the inside. More importantly, when Mark said, "I don't know what the hell I'm doing," he unassumingly issued forth a warning that pursuing one's course in life does not afford any vistas from which to gaze upon the destination and, in that moment of glimpse, gain a sense of orientation vis-à-vis one's present location. Absent such a vantage point, all that we can do is to do what we cannot not do, listening attentively and looking alertly for signs as to what the next step must be, securing our footing best we can. That moment with Mark did not offer me an experience of "the halakha" in the narrow sense of the term, from within, as it were; instead, it offered me my first conscious understanding of what I might term meta-halakha (or perhaps just "halakha" in its deeper sense). I understood what it is to live a life of devotion, an utter devotion that responds to a call but receives no promise of certainty.

My path to the halakha, and most of my journey within its expanses, are intimately related to my decision at age 16 to move to Israel. Roaming the graves of the military cemetery on Mount Herzl in Jerusalem, I looked at the tombstones of fallen soldiers from Israel's War of Independence. I saw the names of women and men—but what struck me over and over again were the ages: some just older than me, some my age, quite a few even younger than I. I understood that I was adult enough to offer my life in devotion. With a clarity that few moments in my life have bestowed,

I understood that if Israel were so important to me that I would begin every day by scouring *The New York Times* for articles about Israel (this was 1986, long before the advent of the Internet), then I needed to be living my life there. I returned to Houston and told my parents that although they would no doubt assume it would be a stage I would outgrow, I was going to move to Israel.

For reasons that I still have trouble deciphering, it was clear to me that I would first do my undergraduate degree in the United States, and only then move to Israel. That decision translated into a long (six-year) limbo period in which I was oriented toward moving to Israel—but not yet there. This often provided cause for anxiety: would my Hebrew be good enough? What would I do when I moved there? When would I serve in the army? Would I be able to make it there? But those haunting questions never burgeoned into a force that caused me to abandon my goal; nor did they convince me to move before the appointed hour had arrived.

In the fall of 1988, during one of the many moments of my anticipatory ponderings, I sat on a bus on an outdoor trip in the Delaware Water Gap with college classmates, reading an article in *The New York Times* about Rabbi Professor David Hartman and the Shalom Hartman Institute that he had founded in Jerusalem to serve as an incubator for new Jewish ideas that grappled with the unprecedented reality and opportunity offered by Jewish autonomy. I stared at his picture, dreaming about finding a home at that Institute, nestled in the heart of Jerusalem, immersing myself in the vital ideas that shape the core of the reality that I could only read about in *The New York Times*. Michael Walzer's thought had convinced me of the need for the connected social critic, and I dreamed that the Shalom Hartman Institute would offer me a base for that work.

I could not have imagined that nine years later I would find myself sitting across from David Hartman in his office, seeking his counsel. I was no longer interested in assuming the role of social critic. Bruria, my wife, had repeatedly leveled a critique of that aspiration, suggesting that the posturing of the critic was distant and aloof, and adding that there existed a more constructive model of engagement and commitment. With time, her words found their way in until they became authentically mine: I had replaced the desire to voice criticism with an aspiration to educate; and, in my teaching, I had integrated, alongside discourse and the discussion of ideas, the power of the נּיגון [*niggun*], the wordless melody. At that point where words break off, run their course, or simply dissipate, the niggun takes over and allows that which eludes words, or can only come after they have been exhausted, to find expression. The niggun allowed for a shift—and lowering—of the student's center of gravity, as engagement of the texts and ideas became more genuine, with less posturing.

Already my greatest teacher, Bruria had taught me that holding fast to my dreams requires a grip loose enough that the dreams can shift and grow, undergoing a transformation from what I thought they were into what they need to become. And so I came to David Hartman's office not as part of a journey of becoming a connected critic; rather, I struggled to determine whether to pursue doctoral studies or to seek rabbinic ordination. I thought that he—because he had both degrees and, to a certain extent, wore both hats (that of the critical thinker and that of the creative rabbinic force)—might offer me insight.

The day before the meeting, however, I nearly canceled it. I knew Hartman—I had taken a course with him at Hebrew University, met with him when writing a paper on his thought, and he had even performed our wedding—but I didn't feel that he knew me well enough to offer anything other than general thoughts about the relative merits of a PhD and rabbinic ordination. Don't cancel, my wife said: you never know where things go.

So the next day I showed up in his office. After telling him why I had come, I had barely begun explaining the considerations for pursuing a doctorate when Hartman interrupted me. Don't go get a doctorate, he enjoined. I was so taken aback by the clarity of his conviction that I asked: then what do you think I should do? Come study with me for a few years, he said, and at the end of the process I'll give you סמיכה [*smikha*] (ordination). If you have a חברותא [*hevruta*] (study partner), he's welcome to join you and I'll give him *smikha* too.

I was caught entirely unprepared by the offer. I thanked him profusely and asked for a few days to consider. I was strongly committed to an egalitarian Judaism; Hartman—less so. At our wedding, I had wanted my wife to give me a ring, but he balked. In the end, he agreed—but it was with hesitation. He had offered to ordain my *hevruta*, and I wondered what he would do if my *hevruta* were a woman. At that time, no Orthodox authorities would ordain women. Though Hartman was a renegade at so many levels—or perhaps *because* of that, I assumed he would not want to enter the fray of fighting that battle. I asked myself whether I would want to receive ordination from someone who would not ordain women, and my intuitive answer was no: I felt that somehow I would be complicit in that wrongdoing by accepting his ordination in such a circumstance.

Then, a couple of days later, Rabbi Hartman, without uttering a word, taught me his first (and perhaps his only) lesson in applied halakha. He had offered me his ordination, I realized, despite the fact that he knew that I was committed to a more egalitarian halakha than he was; how, then, would I, as his student, dare to expect my teacher to conform to *my* understanding of the halakha? This was at once a lesson in personal humility, in teacher–student relations, in pluralism, and in the workings of halakhic change.

I returned to his office a few days later and accepted his invitation, even though I had neither a *hevruta* nor the knowledge that, just a few days ago, had seemed so pivotal to me (whether he would ordain my hevruta if she were a woman). It would take me nearly a year to share my decision to study for rabbinic ordination with anyone other than family and the closest circle of friends. Something about that decision—about the posturing involved in studying in order to be a rabbi, about the superciliousness of placing myself in a position of authority, about the gravitas of being a link in the ongoing interpretation and teaching of Torah—seemed overwhelming to me. And yet, I knew that it was the right decision. I knew this because I had not made the decision: the decision transpired. An internal calling and an external invitation had met.

In the introduction to his seminal book, *A Living Covenant*, Hartman writes of his difficulty in pinpointing a discrete moment at which he received his calling as a rabbi.

> If I answer that it began when I entered *yeshivah* at age five to study Bible and Talmud, they might believe that I am likening myself to Jeremiah, who received his prophetic calling as a child. If I tell them that I never received a calling but was ordained after my teachers concluded that I was intellectually capable of rendering competent decisions regarding what is prohibited and permitted by Jewish law, they might be shocked at meeting a modern version of a Pharisee. .... How could I, they might wonder, preach the word of the Torah without first experiencing God's direct active guidance in my life?[3]

Hartman describes his Jewish journey as a continuum, such that his decision to become a rabbi—a teacher and mediator of the Jewish tradition—was a kind of natural outgrowth of a journey he began in the home in which he grew up. He and I grew up in very different Jewish homes: his becoming a rabbi was a kind of natural extension of his upbringing, whereas mine was a much more effortful one. Like him, I do not identify a moment of "calling" to be a rabbi. Nonetheless, as I mentally traverse the road of my spiritual journey, though I cannot locate "God's direct, active guidance," I can and do locate places and events—beginnings—in which I can identify a kind of keen listening on my part, and a hearing. It is to them that I go back.

A distinct first significant moment stands out clearly: in third grade, I came home from my Jewish elementary school and declared that I wanted to separate meat and dairy. I had been taught that day that according to the laws of כשרות [*kashrut*], meat and dairy must be kept separate, out of sensitivity to the mother, lest we eat her young while drinking her milk. I was touched by the effort to fashion our eating in a way that expressed our sensitivity to animals, even as we ate them. At least that is how I reconstruct and express now the sense I had then. But one thing was clear: I could not stand the dissonance of learning something inspiring or admirable and not giving that idea concrete expression in my lived life. I was (already) refusing to allow for a wedge that divides between Torah and halakha.

But my decision to begin separating dairy and meat was more than a desire to live consistently and more than an attempt to eat ethically. I felt an ineluctable pull to do so. Commanded, perhaps.

By whom? I don't think that I asked that question. And even today, when I experience a similar sense of being commanded, I rarely ask the question—at least not in that way. Instead, I close my eyes and listen hard for the command, to the command. I open them, and then I perform a kind of virtual squint, eyeing the command up and down until my eyes glass over and the command blurs and fades away, and again I can shut my eyes and listen to the command, listen for the command, hear the command. I open my eyes to the world once more, seeing it with a new clarity, and behold, it may well be that the command is a part of that world, it is at home in the world, it belongs to my world.

In third grade, I did not shut my eyes, nor did I listen so intently. But I heard. And with the innocent clarity that only a child of that age can muster, I began separating dairy and meat. That meant for me (and my amazingly compliant parents) that in contrast to the rest of my family, I had one plate and set of utensils for meat and another one for dairy. I was still eating non-kosher meat that had been cooked in potware used jointly for both. So it was "kosher-style," or perhaps better still: incremental kashrut—but that truly was, and is, beside the point. It was a move from where I was, a departure from my comfort zone, a break with my family, a listening and a hearing, and a move toward some communal boundary, even if that community was an "imagined community"—a community of observers with whom I was not (yet) rubbing shoulders or sharing space.[4]

After a few years, my kashrut lapsed, only to resurface again when I was in high school. At about the same time, I found myself staying home on Friday nights even after the conclusion of our family's Shabbat dinner, which included traditional blessings as well as a discussion of Jewish-Torah content, crafted by my father. Perhaps anyone who remembers their adolescent years—and the ruthless, uncompromising desire to fit in—has a sense of what was at stake in my decision to stop meeting friends on Friday night and stay at home instead. But only someone from Texas, who understands the enormity of Friday night high school football, can truly understand the nature of my decision. Though I did not play football, I was still a part of the "in" crowd. So I was voluntarily entering a no-man's zone—a place of isolation that felt more like a nurturing spa than a form of high school exile. On Friday nights, I withdrew from my community of friends and entered into a community that did not yet exist for me in my reality of suburban Houston. In fact, I was not in search of community: I simply had a clarity that the actions of my community of friends didn't belong to me on that day.

Here, too, just as with the kashrut, I struggle in an effort to pin down the nature of the motivation. Did I feel the deep draw of Shabbat *qua* rest? I don't think so. As hard as I worked in high school and into college, I don't think I really *understood* that depth of Shabbat until adulthood. So if it wasn't to rest, and it worked against my social interest—can we rule out, as Yeshayahu Leibowitz would have it, all anthropocentric motivations in my observing this *mitzvah*?[5] Could it have been theocentric? I clearly knew of the Biblical injunction to set aside Shabbat as a day of rest—it is, after all, one of the Ten Commandments. But I think that neither their prominent place nor their injunctive language bore any influence on me. Certainly not at a conscious level. What I can say is that at the deepest level I felt that it would be violative of Shabbat to leave my home and go out after dinner. Or, put positively, it was as if the couch in our den drew me to itself powerfully, and as I sunk into its soft cushions I touched that point of rest, that point of quietude, that central point of vitality, that vital point of centeredness, that the *Sefat Emet*[6] so often describes in his homiletic pieces.

At about the same time, I began laying תפילין [*tefillin*] (phylacteries), incorporating prayer into my morning routine. I had received *tefillin* for my bar mitzvah, but those *tefillin* did then what they're still doing now: collect dust. I found morning prayer when I found the *tefillin* of my maternal grandfather—after whom I am named—in my brother's closet. As I came across them in their tattered, red velour bag, I had a clear sense that they should not be resting in the dark closet in the dark-walled room of my brother who was no longer living at home. It isn't that I felt it was a disservice to or disrespect of my grandfather; after all, when I asked my mom about them, she told me that her father had stopped donning them on a daily basis after learning that his parents, sister, and niece had been killed in the Shoah. In a way that I could not have articulated then, I was seeking a connection to the spiritual realm that I intuitively knew I would not find in my home. Though my mother attended synagogue most *shabbatot*, it was my father's *Weltanschauung* that loomed large in our home: the Jewish people and Jewish culture were of the utmost importance, but the rational conclusion of the problem of evil was that God did not exist. End of discussion.

The irony (linkage? miracle? mystery?) which I discover only upon the very writing of these lines is that I would find the *tefillin* that opened for me the doors of Jewish prayer in the closet of my dear brother Mark, who had already begun to manifest his holy and loyal rebellion against institutional-ized Judaism at the time of his bar mitzvah, when he decided to talk about the problem of evil in his bar mitzvah speech. He was in a sense making good on the promise of my father's "theology," living out what A.D. Gordon called כפירה גדולה [*kefira gedola*]—what we might translate as brave, thoughtful, or even righteous heresy.[7] So I was not exactly right in concluding that I would not find that connection in my home. It was there—hidden away, to be sure, but saved steadfastly by Mark, who, with his intuitive wisdom, tends delicately and tenaciously to the artifacts of life that connect us to this-here-world. And these *tefillin* did just that. As I would wrap their straps of worn black leather around my arm, their varying widths and thicknesses revealed to me the contours of my grandfather's left forearm. They were a daily venture for me into the realm of what Saadia Gaon called the מצוות שמעיות [*mitzvot shim'iyot*], those mitzvot whose telos are not clear to us, or—to translate more precisely—those commandments that we can only—or perhaps must—hear.[8]

I don't know to what degree I can, at present, successfully articulate what transpires for me during my moments of prayer. (In fact, I don't know that the problem is articulation; it may well be with my prayer and my being during those moments.) But I know most certainly that back then, at the age of 16, I could not have expressed what was transpiring. I think that my only moments of reflection and self-awareness were those occasions in which Francisca, my parents' housekeeper, would knock on the door to ask me what I wanted for breakfast, only to send forth a "Con permiso," or

"Perdón" when she realized that I was in a moment of prayer. As our eyes met, and just before she would look down out of consideration and humility, I recognized in her eyes those poles of hunger for something beyond and fullness from the encounter with some such beyond, between which my own eyes, my own being, oscillated during prayer.

The *tefillin* were an impetus to these moments of prayer, but they were more than that. Their spiral around my arm was a physical manifestation of and vehicle for the contours of this contemplative moment: I was literally binding myself up with the leather straps of my grandfather, whose name and whose memory I carry in the world. I was connecting myself to the world where he and his wife, my Bubbe, my maternal grandmother, Rachel Katz, grew up—the world where he used to use them. Theirs was the world of pre-Shoah Eastern Europe, described so powerfully by Heschel in *The Earth Is the Lord's*, and that meant—among other things—a world in which piety remained an ideal that many pursued, in innocence and in sincerity, a world in which Jews were Jewish with the entirety of their beings, even as they felt the rupture of modernity.[9] But this Jewish beyond in turn connected to a not-quite-infinite regression of Jewish beyonds, going all the way back to the Biblical injunction to mark the Jewish covenant with the Divine by these "signs," these "bindings."[10] This trope seemed compelling enough to quiet the not-quite-infinite regression of questions: Why black? Why leather? Why that placement on the forehead? Why *those passages* enclosed within them? Why those passages *enclosed* within them, sealed off, stitched away from the light of day? Why seven times around the forearm? Why the strange configuration around the left hand?

It was my Uncle Daniel who taught me how to put on *tefillin*. My father—through a combination of will and intellectual-spiritual effort—had created a bond of learning to the Jewish past, creating-recovering a link to the Jewish past that he did not receive from his parents.[11] But the area of ritual observance did not allure him, so when I wanted to learn how to put on *tefillin*, my natural turn was to Uncle Daniel, himself an observant Conservative Jew and the grandson of Mordecai Kaplan. Thus, he had been given what I lacked: continuity with the world of Jewish ritual observance, a force so potent that even an act as counterintuitive and concocted as putting on *tefillin* becomes effortless and is perfectly sensible. For my part, I would establish connection—to the Divine, via the world of Jewish observance—only with mindful effort.

My attempts to pray at the synagogue echoed my foray into the world of phylacteries. There, too, I had to overcome a deep-seated inhibition and sense of awkwardness. There, too, I felt ungraceful and unnatural. There, too, I was guided by Uncle Daniel, along with my Aunt Karol and their three children, who—through gentle effort and, even more effectively, with none whatsoever, as they simply lived out their lives—showed me what a lived life of Jewish observance was. The Hebrew נוסח [*nusah*] (language of the prayers), the chanting of the Torah: I watched and listened, trying to make them mine, struggling to achieve a sense of comfort that would allow me to express myself, to do my spiritual seeking, authentically. They had an ease with observance that I sought to emulate. But I was also seeking something else, something other than this comfort, something that I intuitively felt lacking in the (suburban) Judaism that I knew. I identified deeply with the critique of American synagogue Judaism that I would read a dozen or so years later in Heschel's *Man's Quest for God*. "Nothing unpredictable must happen to the person who prays," writes Heschel, bemoaning the fact that "[c]ongregants preserve a respectful distance between the liturgy and themselves."[12] I was striving for some kind of beyond, pining for a connection to some unarticulated, undifferentiated sense of the numinous.[13] The words and rotes of tradition were not constitutive of it; they were the vessels into which I would enter to travel that uncharted territory. Therefore, over the course of my high school years and especially into my first years in university, when I found myself assuming some ritual of "piety" that went beyond my cousins' practice, I felt a double pang of inauthenticity: first, that I (still) couldn't do what they did naturally and authentically; and second, that I had the audacity to take upon myself a greater level of observance than them, to search for some deeper connection.

At one level, then, my journey into the world of halakhic observance was an exploration of ritual. My experimentation with rituals was like entering a dressing room and slipping on different items of clothing. Sometimes I could try them out with minimal effort, slipping them on over the clothes I was already wearing. But sometimes donning them required more effort, as they had to come in the stead of my existent clothing. Still at other times, even slipping them on seemed too effortful and I would just hold them up in front of me as I stared into the mirror. And when I would try on these various "garments," I would, more often than not, experience that sense of discomfort that one so often experiences in fitting rooms: too tight there, too low there, too loose there. Even the clothes that will eventually fit well need to be broken in, and upon first wearing seem unnatural, stiff. My observance of mitzvot were these garments of clothing, this לבוש [*levush*] (garment) in the deep Hassidic sense according to which they are "merely" shells, vessels in which to contain and through which to channel the ebb and flow of divine–human current.[14] In a way that I didn't understand—and, had I understood, wouldn't have been able or willing to express—I was searching to tap into that current.

Heschel called mitzvot prayers in the form of action[15]—thus bringing to the fore the way in which, through the contours of the halakhically lived life, we are constantly endeavoring to weave out of our life's moments a fabric of connection to the divine. Despite Heschel's protestations to the contrary, in my experience there are, along the edifice of halakhic observance, quite a few cracks and crevices where you can go in and hide—for an extended period—from the light of the encounter with the Divine. But there are some moments that simply cannot be dragged into the dark, shadowy area of the denial of divine presence. Prayer is one of those moments. That is precisely why Leibowitz tries to empty the words of prayer of all of their meaning, claiming that the words of the prayer book have no privileged status: as he declares in his characteristically provocative fashion, had the sages ordained that we read the Jerusalem phone book as the silent עמידה [ amida] prayer, it would be equally meaningful from a theological perspective.[16] Leibowitz is off, for he's failed to recognize the function of language in prayer. No longer translucent in the way that philosophy would have them be, the stylized words of prayer do not endeavor to reflect or describe reality, not even the reality of the God whom we address. Rather, they are generative, beckoning the person engaged in a moment of worship to actualize a reality different from the existent one. Our utterance of words of prayer is the initial grumbling—the sputtering, choked, beginning—of a different reality. What Leibowitz and Heschel shared was an appreciation of the significance of those prayerful moments in which the halakhic deed is an undeniably explicit attempt to address the One. Leibowitz tried to drag even those moments of address into a kind of theological ("theocentric") void, while Heschel grants to each halakhic act the theological intensity of the moment of prayer.

It was those intensely, undeniably spiritual avenues of expression that attracted me. Concurrently, they disarmed me: not only because in them I ventured into unfamiliar territory, but largely because they brought me into the territory of the ineffable. It was not that I lost my footing on the firm ground on which I was used to treading—that of words and concepts as a part of an analytic understanding of reality. Rather, it was that suddenly it had been reduced to *merely* the ground that I stepped on; it was not the entirety of my experience. There was air to breathe, there were things to see, to hear, and to touch; conversations to have; and prayers and *niggunim* to sing. As I would come to understand years later by reading Rosenzweig, thickly lived experience and the prolepsis contained in devotional moments offered me access to, awareness of, and understanding of new depths and new elements of reality.[17] But I would have to learn to trust them.

At college, the solitary wanderings that I had embarked upon from my parents' home in the suburban spiritual desert of Houston interfaced with a living Jewish community of peers.

*Kabbalat Shabbat* and *zemirot* at Princeton's kosher dining hall on Friday nights were my first experiences of the way in which communal prayer and song have the power to generate a holiness that envelops those in its presence. I had to overcome many levels of discomfort in order to find my way over to the men's section of the makeshift synagogue: I was unfamiliar with many of the prayers and most of the melodies; I felt disconnected from the observant, East Coast Jews in whose midst I sat; and I had to ignore the constant chatter of voices inside my head that scoffed at the irrational—dare I say primitive?—enthusiasm of prayer. Yet I was drawn there anyway. The prayer would wash over me, carrying me to an open expanse. Even more: its cohortative[18] quality drew out my own voice—not my singing voice, which I already knew, but an unfamiliar voice: my voice of prayer. I was lifted up by these communal moments, but not carried away: despite their strong allure, I knew that I was not part of that community in a deeper sense. Their halakha was not mine, for my theology—entirely inchoate as it was—was not theirs.

Even more arresting for me than prayer and *zemirot* at the dining hall were Shabbat meals at the table of my Hillel rabbi and his wife, Eddie and Merle Feld. Precisely because we shared a lovingly critical sensibility in our Jewish posture, our theological positions held open the promise of shared ground. And at a deep level, *that* startled me, for the foundational role of belief in their lives was unabashed. Unguarded and off-balance, I could only profess to myself that they had inducted me into the world of holy time. They were (and are) children of the 1960s, but it was not merely their long hair, their turtleneck sweaters, or the décor of their home that thrust me into a time warp. It was around their Shabbat table—especially their dinner table—that their presence brought me into the possibility of time's elasticity. When they sang to each other before Kiddush—אשת חיל [*Eshet Ḥayil*] (a woman of valor) and מי האיש [*Mi ha-ish*] (who is the man)—they were together in an intimacy that was so powerful that I felt violative by being in the space in which they had invited me to inhabit. As one of my Jewish dorm mates once remarked, there was a sense around their Shabbat table that at any given moment the plates may well start levitating. It was so palpable that my dorm mate, who was not especially inclined to things spiritual, offered the observation and I, who was inclined but also quite frightened by them, seemed not only to tolerate the atmosphere, but to relish it, to long for it. Of course, I knew them both during the week, as well—and then their deliberate rhythm nearly always left me impatient, desirous of condensing the long pauses between their words so as to speed up conversation. But around their Shabbat table, time had a different contour—one that was not reducible to the pace of their words. Conversation was meditative, the expanse between people around the table no longer a gulf of separation but a shared space to inhabit. The food itself was a focal point, while eating became a mindful, even sacred endeavor, but at the same time it was an invitation to and vehicle for moments of soulful interpersonal contact. I entered into those holy spaces and experienced the way in which time can expand, the kind of redemptive way in which, as Rosenzweig describes, the present moment can assume weight.[19]

Coming home always offers a strange mixture of the comfort of the returning to our familiar stomping ground with the stifling sense of needing to contract our expanded selves in order to fit into the small space which once contained us. The return to my parents' Shabbat dinner table was just this: I relished that warm area of light that had introduced me into the world of Shabbat, and I wanted to bring back with me, into their dining room, the world of *niggunim* and *zemirot* that I had begun to explore and relish. There was no room. My parents—in their respectful, loving, parental posture—were willing to try to carve out space for me: but I learned intuitively that the power of the *niggun* could only be released when it is shared singing. Even when my family members joined in, my singing was solitary, for it came from a different place in me, from a place of soulful longing that was in גלות [*galut*], in exile, at their table.

But my budding adult spirituality—distinct as it was from the highly intellectual Jewish experience of my parents' home—never "floated off" into the ether of some mystical, or quasi-mystical, experience.[20] My critical faculties remained intact. They were not—and are not—sandbags that kept the spiritual balloon from reaching its high. Rather, they offered a stable framework of two moments—before and after—in which religious experience could transpire. Prior to the experience, they were the force that shaped my openness to, my readiness for, what was to occur. As William James wrote, "[w]hat is called our 'experience' is almost entirely determined by our habits of attention."[21] After the experience, they provided the power that could verify the authenticity of what I had undergone. How long that moment of experience would last varied. But the three moments were inextricably linked, and one without the other was as unsatisfying as a sandwich with just the bread or just the filling.

Perhaps the final signpost on the part of my journey that led me onto the major highway that I am still traveling was my initial encounter with the subject of gender and halakha. It was for me then, as it is now, an area in which the gap—and tension—between the lived experience and the reflective moments surrounding that experience is the greatest. For precisely this reason, it illustrates the dynamic and complex relationship between these two parts of the sandwich.

It took my wife a long time to believe me when I told her that my commitment to egalitarian halakha was not "ideology." Feminist ideas surely shaped the way in which I experienced events; how could they not? And yet, no experienced event can be trumped by ideological commitment. My egalitarian sentiment came from a different, more intuitive place in me. It emerged from an impulse well known to Rabbi Mordechai Lainer of Izbica (the Izbicer Rebbe): in the face of a situation in which the individual feels that the authentic command of the Divine demands a violation of the established halakha, the rebbe from Izbica did not summarily dismiss this inclination. Rather, he demanded that the individual take that voice seriously, subjecting it to a thorough self-probing, בירור [beirur], in order to clarify its staying power and its legitimacy.[22]

The critical moment in my self-probing dates back to one of those Shabbatot in which I was back in Houston from Princeton. At the traditional minyan of my parents' Conservative synagogue, I found myself seated between my college girlfriend, a native of New York who had attended a liberal Orthodox day school through twelfth grade, and my Bubbe Rachel, a stalwart of the minyan. Seating was mixed, but since this was the "traditional" minyan, only men were allowed up on the בימה [bima] (elevated platform) to assume a role in the ceremony. With the same acuity that dogs display when we go over to pet them in order to lure them to the vet, I could feel that the גבאי [gabbai] (prayer organizer), as he was walking down the aisle, was headed our way. I always try to disappear instantaneously when approached by the gabbai, as I find it tremendously difficult to expose myself publicly in intimate moments of worship. As he greeted all three of us, leaning over toward me, I cringed for a different reason. He asked me to open the ark.

If he had asked me to do anything more complex than that—something requiring fluid Hebrew or the likes—I would have had to admit right there that either of the women between whom I was sitting would have been better qualified than I to perform the task. I couldn't quite claim that regarding opening the ark. And yet, the affront seemed so deep that I experienced the question as a blow. While my girlfriend was demonstrably insulted, my Bubbe was not. But that was not because the absurdity of it was lost on her; rather, she viewed it with a kind of smirk of resignation that she had been born into a time when women were not full participants in Jewish ritual.

As I reflected upon that incident in the days and weeks that followed, trying to process its meaning—the meaning of the *gabbai*'s refusal to ask my grandmother or girlfriend to open the ark, their respective reactions, and my reaction—I found myself returning again and again to a conversation that I had had with my parents, both of whom had grown up in the racially segregated South. I asked them how they had reacted to separate fountains and seating for whites and "colored" people. They both looked at me with blank faces. Hard as it was for them to comprehend at the time of my asking—and it was even harder to explain this to others—during that period, they didn't think anything of it at all. That was the reality, and the only reality, that they knew. As I processed and reprocessed my experience at the traditional minyan in light of my parents' experience amid racial segregation, I found myself profoundly oriented in two ways.

First, I gained a sense of clarity regarding the way in which our experience—of justice, of spirituality, of segregation, of inequality, of humanity, of ourselves—is conditioned by the outward reality that confronts us, thus shaping and, in so doing, limiting our perspective. In part, this means that what is other than our reality—but in close proximity to it—can shift and become "imaginable." But it also means that what is too far away from our reality becomes unimaginable as a result of the distance. I realized that the possibilities for gender equality were limited, first and foremost, by our imaginations.

Second, I somehow internalized the opportunity—and obligation—to view moments in their historical perspective, as part of longer processes and trajectories. Just as I looked at my parents with some mixture of disbelief and disappointment as they told me that they did not question their reality enough to wonder about its racial injustice, I anticipated that my actions would be subjected to the same critical scrutiny by my future children; I would have to give an accounting of my choices and actions, those chosen mindfully and those "chosen" blindly by routine. Together, these two reflections shaped my experience of halakhic gender space such that my soul simply has no way to serve the Divine, to travel through sacred devotional grounds, along rigidly determined lines of gender.

This inability is no doubt colored by and emergent from my reflective self—that is, my thoughts and value commitments as I process and develop them consciously in reaction to my experiences in this world. But thorough, repeated reflection and self-probing—though capable of orienting us to experience of the world, opening up certain experiential possibilities while limiting others—can never replace or override the raw power of genuine, grounded experience. This, of course, is why the most precious conversations and moments of interaction frequently occur at the most unexpected times: on the way to the airport at the end of a visit, standing in the stairwell just before saying goodnight. It is also why—much to my chagrin as a father— parents can plan an amazing family outing, but we cannot force our children to have a good time. There is something truly miraculous, truly revelatory, truly mysterious about the experience as it unfolds and we dwell in it.

That is not to say that that very moment of experience is somehow entirely discrete and discontinuous from all moments leading up to its cusp. The I who enters into and undergoes that space and moment is, of course, the I who is emergent from every experience–thought–emotion– encounter, the forgotten and the remembered, the conscious and the unconscious, which brought me to the brink of this very moment. We are who we are—and, to a great extent, who we may still become—because of the sum total of our past experiences. But, however powerful the past's grip on us may be in shaping how we experience the world, there remains a horizon of experience that is fundamentally and powerfully undetermined, as the future explodes uncontrollably into and onto the present moment. If we are open to it and honest about it after it has passed us by—we may find ourselves surprised and transformed by it.

And so it is that the experience of sitting between my girlfriend and my Bubbe on that day impacted me and my subsequent experiences, leading to my refusal—or perhaps inability—to allow halakhic behavior to assume rigidly defined gender lines. It is far from being a matter of "ideology" for me. Rather, I left that experience with an orientation, a grounding upon which each subsequent experience treads. Each experience holds within it a sacred reality that has yet to unfold, bursting upon—and often rubbing against—the stylized possibilities that once seemed exhaustive.

\*   \*   \*

The Talmud teaches that it is the father's obligation to circumcise his son. If he fails to do so, the community must assume responsibility. And if they fail, the child, upon entering adulthood and becoming an agent, must circumcise himself.[23] The Talmudic authors/legislators were no doubt aware of the grimace of pain that such an image would conjure: in this way, they meant to convey the rawness of the painful, arduous journey that a person must embark upon in order to enter the fold from without.

I was exposed to Jewish ritual by my parents and community; but I would enter the world of halakhic living—a theologically-infused, existentially-committed praxis—through my own efforts. Over the course of this chapter, I have tried to describe some of my points of entry and initiation. In my רב מובהק [*rav muvhak*], my predominant teacher, Rabbi David Hartman, I found someone who was born into the halakhic world. That is why, after a few years in the field as a rabbi, he could conclude that the task of a rabbi is to provoke questions, not to offer halakhic answers.[24] And that is why, when he walked into the room in which my hevruta and I were studying the *Mishnah Berurah*, Rabbi Yisrael Meir Kagan's legal codex based on Rabbi Yosef Karo's *Shulkhan Arukh*, he would express disappointment that we were busying ourselves with the minutiae of the halakha. But my way to the halakha was outside in, so my perspective of and posturings toward the halakha were necessarily different from those of my beloved teacher. The journey that begins from the periphery, while in many senses disadvantaged, also offers a certain kind of privileged vantage point—precisely because of its point of origin, and because of the road traversed to gain entry. Rosenzweig, in the dedication of the Lehrhaus in Frankfurt, invited the unique contributions of those who came to the fold of Jewish learning from without, insisting that the learners bring their full biographies with them: only in this way would Torah emerge.[25] So, too, I would assert, with the Torah of the halakha: in the upcoming pages, I can only offer an understanding of halakha to the extent that it rests upon, and is emergent from, my way to the halakha.

At one of the meetings of a seminar on the subject of women and halakha, Rabbi Hartman, visibly impatient with the conservative positions on issues of gender equality espoused by the established halakhic authorities, encouraged the women who had presented position papers to stop waiting for the rabbis to issue halakhic ruling that would effectuate change. Just act differently! he enjoined. Disregard the halakhic norm, he demanded, and you'll see the rabbinic "authorities" follow suit. They will have to follow suit, for the halakha cannot exist absent of its committed observers, irrespective of rabbinic will. After the seminar, I approached Rabbi Hartman and shared with him my sense that, for the audience to whom he spoke, there was a place for a paradigm shift within halakhic literature: existent halakhic rulings were based on conceptions of authority and autonomy that were no longer relevant for many Jews who were deeply committed to halakha. What was needed was a new genre of halakhic literature, one based on appeal. In a certain sense, the remainder of this work is a prolegomena to such a literature.

## NOTES

1. Martin Buber, *I and Thou*, trans. Walter Kaufman (New York: Charles Scribner's Sons, 1970), 78–79.
2. Franz Rosenzweig, *Understanding the Sick and the Healthy: A View of World, Man, and God*, trans. Nahum Glatzer (Cambridge: Harvard University Press, 1999), 39ff.
3. David Hartman, *A Living Covenant: the Innovative Spirit in Traditional Judaism* (New York: The Free Press, 1985), 7.
4. The term "imagined communities" was coined by Benedict Anderson in his 1983 book of the same title, in which he argues that the nation "is *imagined* because the members of even the smallest nation will never know most of their fellow-members, meet them, or even hear of them, yet in the minds of each lives the image of their communion. . . . In fact, all communities larger than primordial villages of face-to-face contact (and perhaps even these) are imagined" Benedict Anderson, *Imagined Communities* (New York: Verso, 2002), 6.
5. Yeshayahu Leibowitz, the twentieth-century Israeli philosopher of Judaism, argues that performance of the commandments of the Torah for any reason other than the mere fact of their being divine commandments is tantamount to idolatry. "Whoever regards the service of God as a means for fulfilling his wishes – be they 'life, children, or nutrition' or the satisfaction of an emotional need . . . is seeking his own advantage and not applying himself to the service of God" Yeshayahu Leibowitz, *Judaism, Human Values, and the Jewish State*, ed. Eliezer Goldman (Cambridge, Harvard University Press, 1992), 43.
6. Rabbi Yehudah Aryeh Leib Alter of Ger, Poland, 1847–1905.
7. A.D. Gordon, "The Human Being and Nature," in *Selected Writings*, ed. S.H Bergman and A.L. Shohat (Jerusalem: The Zionist Library of the World Zionist Organization, 1982), 56 [Hebrew].

8. According to Saadia Gaon, *Mitzvot shim'iyot* are ritual-based *mitzvot* that do not in themselves have a reason, and if not for the Torah, their prohibitions would not be known. See Saadia Gaon, *Beliefs and Opinions*, trans. Samuel Rosenblatt (New Haven: Yale University Press, 1967), Article Three, Chapter Two.

9. Abraham Joshua Heschel, *The Earth Is the Lord's: The Inner World of the Jew in Eastern Europe* (USA: Farrar, Straus & Giroux, 1978).

10. Deuteronomy 6:8.

11. Leon Wiener Dow, "Circumcising Yourself," *The Reconstructionist*, Fall 2007.

12. Abraham Joshua Heschel, *Man's Quest for God*, (Santa Fe: Aurora Press, 1996), 49–50.

13. Rudolph Otto, *The Idea of the Holy*, (Oxford: Oxford University Press, 1958), 1–11.

14. See, for example, Shneur Zalman of Liadi, *The Tanya*, Part One, Chapter Four.

15. Heschel, *Man's Quest for God*, 93–96.

16. Yeshayahu Leibowitz, "Prayer," in *Judaism, The Jewish People, and the State of Israel* (Tel Aviv: Schocken, 1979), 386–390 [Hebrew].

17. Franz Rosenzweig, *The Star of Redemption* (Notre Dame, IN: Notre Dame Press, 1985), 272–275, 289–297.

18. Ibid., 231–232.

19. Ibid., 65.

20. Ibid., 207–208.

21. William James, *Psychology: Briefer Course* in *Works of William James*, ed. Frederick Burkhardt, Fredson Bowers, and Ignas K. Skrupsekelis (Cambridge, MA: Harvard University Press, 1984), 156.

22. Rabbi Mordechai Lainer of Iczbiza, *Mei HaShiloah*, Part I, *Lekh Lekha*, 7a–7b; Ibid., *Ḥukat*, 52a; Ibid., *Pinḥas*, 54a.

23. B.T. Tractate Kiddushin 39a.

24. David Hartman, *The God Who Hates Lies: Confronting and Rethinking Jewish Tradition*, with Charlie Buckholtz (Woodstock, VT: Jewish Lights, 2011), 28ff.

25. At his speech at the dedication ceremony, Rosenzweig stated: "All of us to whom Judaism, to whom being a Jew, has again become the pivot of our lives ... we all know that in being Jews we must not give up anything, not renounce anything, but lead everything back to Judaism. From the periphery back to the center; from the outside, in. ... Just glance at our prospectus. You will find, listed among others, a chemist, a physician, a historian, an artist, a politician. Two-thirds of the teachers are persons who, 20 or 30 years ago, in the only century when Jewish learning had become the monopoly of specialists, would have been denied the right of teaching in a Jewish House

of Study. They have come together here as Jews. . . . Whoever teaches here –
and I believe I may say this in the name of all who are teaching here – knows
that in teaching here he need sacrifice nothing of what he is" Franz
Rosenzweig, "Upon Opening the Jüdisches Lehrhaus," in Franz
Rosenzweig, *On Jewish Learning*, edited by Nahum Glazer (New York:
Schocken, 1955), 98–99.

# CHAPTER 2

# Saying, Writing, Doing

**Abstract** This chapter brings into sharp focus the privileged status of action. After an exploration of two "moments" of language—speaking and writing—Wiener Dow connects these two stylizations of language to the Written Torah (The Hebrew Bible) and the Oral Torah (rabbinic literature). The rabbis, he argues, crafted a unified Torah that included both aspects of language, viewing the principal charge of Torah as allowing the eternal, commanding words of the Divine to achieve instantiation in the finite world. The infinite interpretive possibility of the words of Torah yields to an uncompromising insistence that their meaning be realized and expressed through discrete action. Halakha, so conceived, is a response to the Divine in deed. As such, it is interpersonal, creating a shared language of deed and establishing community.

**Keywords** Oral Torah and Written Torah • Language, speech, and action • Buber and Rosenzweig • Spoken and written word • Wissenschaft and Torah • Divine speech • Aggadah and halakha

As we cleaned up the room after the pre-Passover learning program that "Ta Shma," an organization that I had founded devoted to pluralistic, informal Jewish education, had conducted in conjunction with Hillel at Tel Aviv University, I found on a desk in the corner of the room a green piece of paper folded over many times. I realized immediately who had been

© The Author(s) 2017

L. Wiener Dow, *The Going*,

https://doi.org/10.1007/978-3-319-68831-2_2

sitting in that desk. I had attended the session in an administrative capacity and, as I observed the two educators co-teaching, I glanced around the room to appraise who, in my estimation, was there out of genuine interest in the learning, and who was there for the free pizza. I had located the young man who sat disinterestedly in the corner as someone who had, without a doubt, come for the pizza. As more students entered the room during the course of the learning session, I eyed the young man with a measure of pity, for he had been boxed into the corner, and his potential post-pizza escape route had vanished. Once the learning part of the session was in full swing—and the pizza long gone—the two educators offered a metaphorical, Hassidic understanding of חמץ [*hametz*], leaven, as those parts of our self that have become inflated and need to be destroyed.[1] They distributed small green pieces of paper and asked each student to write down two pieces of *hametz* that they wished to extirpate from themselves. It was one of these pieces of paper that I had found in that corner seat. I didn't know the student by name and had no reason to assume I would encounter him again, so I felt free to unfold the note and read its contents. I was nothing short of flabbergasted to find written inside in unsteady writing:

smoking
using people

The person who I had assumed, with utter certainty, to have attended just for the pizza, had in fact engaged in—or been engaged by—Torah study in all of its fierce power. The spoken words of Torah had penetrated and touched him, issuing forth a (written) response, one that revealed a genuine aspiration to self-transformation. To this day, I keep that folded green note in my bag, with me at all times.

This story holds many levels of truth: about our inability to judge people and situations (and my own unjustified alacrity in arriving at such judgments); about the potential of educational moments to reach well beyond what the eye can see; and about the opportunities (and pitfalls) of using educational "accessories" and tools in order to get students "in the door" and in order to spur students to introspection. But the reason that I still keep that folded note in my bag is to remind me about the elusive and mysterious power of the spoken word. Precisely because maintaining trust in that power is so supremely difficult, I grasp at the lasting, written traces of the transient spoken word's power.

What is this elusive and mysterious power? Precisely because, as Rosenzweig pointed out, it is nourished by time—it is *alive*, and herein lies its force.[2] What does it mean for the spoken word to be alive? It means that it issues forth from a living creature: it enters the world as the air is cut by a mouth, attached to the face, of a person. It also means that it emerges in time. And for these reasons, it can die: for what is death if not the proof of the creature's transience, of time's dominion. More about the death of the spoken word shortly.

To be alive, truly alive, infused with vitality, also means to be present. Here, "presence" carries its dual spatiotemporal meaning: to have a palpable effect on those in proximity, and to dwell in that fleeing moment that is no-longer-past and not-yet-future. The spoken word does just that: it dwells in that space between the interlocutors, forming a tissue that binds them. It is directed to someone, to someone specific, and in it the speaker literally reveals herself, thrusting into the outside world those thoughts and feelings that dwell(ed) in her; and the listener, in her listening, ushers in the revealed depth of the speaker, enabling the speaker to be present for her and to her. What was previously hidden now has a face—a face from which it emerged, and it is addressed to a specific face, overpowering the ravine of distance and difference that separates them. Each in her own way, each from her own vantage point and visage, shares in the word.

The immediate lifespan of the spoken word is astoundingly short: as the air passes through the vocal chords and our mouth, it forms the sounds that, almost instantaneously, the listener hears; and then it is no more. But the spoken word, of course, can continue to reverberate even after it has disappeared, in much the same way that a person's presence can continue to be felt even after she has left a room. Precisely because of its potency in establishing connective presence in the manner described earlier, the spoken word reverberates, and its echoes continue to wield a powerful impact. We might even say they continue to linger, sounding their voice after they are gone, and we continue to "converse" with our interlocutor long after the conversation has terminated.

"Rabbi Yoḥanan says in the name of Rabbi Shimon ben Yehoẓadak: anyone in whose name an halakhic teaching is quoted in this world – that person's lips speak from the grave, as it is said: 'causing the lips of those sleeping to move' (Song of Songs 7:10)."[3] Rabbi Yoḥanan and Rabbi Shimon ben Yehoẓadak—both of whom are speaking to us at this very moment—understand the profound way in which the spoken word, and with it, its speaker, can become present again, breaking through and transcending barriers of place and time, so mighty is its power of presence.

And yet, despite this very power, and intimately related to it, the spoken word can also die. Rabbi Yoḥanan's and Rabbi Shimon ben Yehoẓadak's words come in the context of a discussion of תחיית המתים [tehiyyat ha-meitim], the resurrection of the dead. Although we normally think of "resurrection of the dead" to mean dead bodies or souls returning to life, Rabbi Yehoshua ben Levi suggests a radically different understanding of the concept:

> A person who sees his friend for the first time in thirty days says the blessing, "Blessed is the One who has granted us the force of life and existence and allowed us to reach this day." [A person who sees his friend for the first time] in twelve months [says] "Blessed is the One who resuscitates the dead."

When we have not seen someone for 12 months, says Rabbi Yehoshua ben Levi, that person is dead for us. Her existence, her life force, her presence no longer flows into the basin of our existence. Although that living person may reenter our lives, bursting into our consciousness and coming to life—she may well not do so, and if she does not, her absence is, from our perspective, her death.

So, too, the spoken word: when it no longer reverberates in the echo chamber of our consciousness and conversations, it dies its death. This is not an instantaneous combustion, a total and sudden negation of its prior existence. Rather, like our bodily death in which we decompose and are reabsorbed into the earth, becoming a part of the ecosystem anew as our former cells find a regenerated existence, the spoken word is broken down and absorbed into us, into our consciousness, and its constituent components nourish our cells and are absorbed by them as their life force transforms into, and is absorbed by, an entirely new existence.

And yet for all of the spoken word's power, despite its ability to rise again to life or, short of that, metamorphose into a new form of life, our fear of its death looms large. Just as the fear of our own death animates so many of our motives and decisions, conscious and unconscious, our awareness and fear of the spoken word's transience foster a kind of inimical suspicion and underestimation of its potency. We assume that its circumscription in place and time leaves it atrophied, subjected to the vagaries of human memory. Out of this desperation and mistrust, we turn to the written word.

The written word has precisely what the spoken word lacks: permanence, immutability, and a wide reach. In stark contrast to the spoken one, the written word has no regard for time. It speaks to no one; instead, it speaks to anyone. And it awaits no reply. In this sense, it speaks at, not to. Because it has no regard for the particularity of its reader, it can address a wide audience. Its black letters promise neither to fade nor to change. Chances are, it will not leave the reader's presence and return with force, as the spoken word does. It will wait patiently, silently, steadfastly, until the reader decides to pull it off the shelf and open the book again. True, it may surprise us and burst in expectedly, an uninvited guest who imposes a presence upon us. But our relationship with it has overtones of power and struggle, and it is saturated by our asserted autonomy: we read it only because we choose to cast our glance upon it, and we can, at any moment, shelve it, silencing its nonexistent mouth. It remains exactly what it is and what it was before we read it, unaffected by our glance, our exclamation, or our written response. Regardless of our affect toward it, the black letters of the written word promise to remain unaltered. They will neither change nor fade over time. They promise permanence; therein lies their appeal.

The spoken word holds no such promise. Though it can burrow its way into the deepest recesses of the consciousness of the conversant, we don't fully trust it. Bound as it is to time, we fear—and know—that its ephemeral nature means that it will, quite literally, vanish into thin air, leaving "only" its traces, its echoes. And so, we write or seek other ways to transform the spoken word into something that promises permanence.

Returning to the green note that I carry in my bag, I can recast what I wrote earlier: I hold on to it not because of the power of the spoken word, but rather because I do not fully trust this power. The spoken word has unique capability, and yet we do not fully trust it: nestled in the interstices between these two statements lies the key to understanding the complex, sometimes troubled, and always dynamic relationship between the written and the spoken words.

*   *   *

What we roughly identify as "Judaism" is, for all intents and purposes, the offspring of "Rabbinic Judaism"—that is, the rabbis who lived in the Land of Israel and in Babylon between the years 0 and 550 CE (as well as the efforts for another 200 years of rabbis who, with their editorial hands, crafted into their polished forms what we refer to as the Babylonian Talmud).[4] And the cornerstone or Rabbinic Judaism is the assertion—or shall I say invention—of the compound nature of the Torah, consisting of the Written Torah and the Oral Torah. The relationship between them, like the relationship between written and spoken words, is dynamic and complex. In its contours we find not only Judaism as we know it, but the ongoing Jewish conversation between humans and the Divine.

God, as it were, didn't trust the spoken word either. So God gave the Written Torah (God spoke, Moses wrote). And when God (and God's prophets) stopped speaking entirely, the Sages opened their mouths and filled the vacuum. Created in God's image, they, too, worried about the long-term viability of an Oral Torah, and so they wrote theirs down (without rebranding it). Rabbis have been writing ever since, but they've been "merely" jotting down theological reflections or summarizing halakhic decisions: their written words may be "Torah"—teaching—broadly conceived, but they are not constitutive of *the* Torah.

These nine lines provide an irreverent yet largely accurate summary of the concept of Torah regnant in traditional Jewish circles. As my rabbi and teacher David Hartman would say: In Orthodox Judaism, original sin is being born *later*. The further we are from Sinai, the more remote we are from God and the divine word, the less holy we are, the less justified we are to dare halakhically or theologically.[5] Our predecessors—merely by virtue of their relative proximity to the uttering of God's word—enjoy privileged status. God's spoken word was written down, and when the holy sages of rabbinic Judaism had uttered their last words, and Ravina and Rav Ashi had cast the Babylonian Talmud into its edited-and-eventually-to-be-written form, they siphoned off all future innovation, excluding the possibility of an ongoing record of our theological conversation, as it were. Written Word 2, Oral Word 0. Game Over.

That is not to say, of course, that there is no record of our ongoing theological conversations. In fact, *Hasidism* did that quite well, as students would write down the Torah (teaching) their teachers had taught on the previous Shabbat. And yet, as radical—halakhically and theologically—as *Hasidism* sometimes was, it never contained a thoroughgoing attempt to redefine Torah itself in the way that the rabbis did. These recordings were understood and integrated as *torot*, the teachings of the *rebbe*, but not as *Torah* per se, not constitutive of the body of Torah. The Oral and Written Torah remained sealed gates.

The rabbis' radical innovation is *enabled* by the license they grant themselves as creators of Oral Torah. But the innovation itself, their astonishing accomplishment, is to craft the two Torahs together into one. By fusing the written and the spoken words, the rabbis claim the possibility that the eternal, immutable word and the word of the moment can be one. That is, the eternal word can speak now, and that potential is enabled by the constancy of the ever-new spoken word.

In the beginning was the spoken word. And here we must be precise: "in the beginning" means that the speaking of the word and the very notion of time are inseparable. Thus located within temporality, the divinely-spoken word brings the entirety of existence into being. After speaking the world into existence, the Divine converses with human beings many more times, but the crescendo of the clamor takes place, of course, at Sinai, where the thunder of the words is so powerful that the mountain shakes and the words are visible.[6] As if they were written. Moses writes some of the words down right then, saving others for later, when conditions for writing improve— when there will be better lighting and less background noise. But even in those ideal conditions, Moses himself, who spoke with the Divine face-to-face, can't manage to write down everything. The written word has an edge, an outer limit, and it is demarcated by—his death.

That is both the plain meaning of the Biblical text *and* a rabbinic hermeneutic elevation of the text into the realm of philosophical-theological discourse—and the rabbis of the Talmud effortlessly vouch for both of these truths of the text through a disagreement between Rabbi Yehuda and Rabbi Shimon.[7]

Rabbi Yehuda insists that Joshua wrote the last eight verses of the Torah, for how could it be, he asks, that Moses speaks of his death in the past tense? Yet Rabbi Shimon is willing to allow for this paradox, for the alternative is unfathomable. Could it be, he asks, that the Torah—the divine word as spoken to Moses—is missing even a single letter? The Torah as we have it must, for Rabbi Shimon, represents a transmission of the divine word of uncompromised fidelity. Nonetheless, acknowledging the power of Rabbi Yehuda's challenge, Rabbi Shimon suggests that the modus operandi changed for the last eight verses: up until then, God had spoken and Moses wrote. For the last eight verses, however, God spoke and Moses wrote while crying.

Rabbi Yehuda thus offers a sensibility that reveals the limits of the encounter between finite creatures and the Infinite One, and death—the ultimate sign of our finitude—as the line of demarcation between the infinite possibilities of the spoken word and the finite structure the word can assume in its written form. We simply cannot record it all, in much the same way that, as Stephen Wright has joked, we cannot have a life-size map of the United States or, as Borges wrote in "Funes, the Memorious," we cannot maintain memories of total and infinite fidelity to the occurrence itself.[8] Rabbi Shimon, by contrast, argues for a more robust possibility of transmittal, but even he admits that in the last eight verses, a tear is shed during the process of writing down the spoken word of the Divine, and that means: human emotion, indeed humanity itself, begins to encroach, and the flowing of tears indicates here what it always indicates—that the depths of the human experience cannot be expressed in words.[9] As the tears well up in the eyes of Moses, they blur his view of the letters below—and, perhaps, as they fall to the parchment, they discolor or smear the black letters written there. Even Rabbi Shimon—the same Rabbi Shimon, of course, who prefers learning Torah in the cave to living it out in the world and who wishes that he had two mouths, one to speak Torah continuously and one to eat and drink[10]—even Rabbi Shimon admits that the writing of the spoken word of the Divine is an act of power and violence, of limitation, of distortion.

God presumably knew this, but had no choice other than to leave behind a written Torah, a kind of "I was here" graffiti, lest the stubborn and faithless people of Israel doubt the power of the Divine's spoken word. The rabbis, created in the image of the Divine, would eventually write down their spoken words, too, but their first task was to transform the written word back into a spoken one. As we saw in the disagreement between Rabbi Yehuda and Rabbi Shimon, they are keenly aware of the way in which the human and the divine elements of Torah are wedded together indissolubly. The spoken word of the Divine seeks its listeners, and/but its listeners must set those words in writing in order to establish their absolute nature. But the rabbis understood that more important than their absolute nature was their infinite nature: they are a constantly flowing spring, welling up ever anew from the depths.

And so, inverting a verse from Jeremiah (23:29) that cautions against false prophets, they likened the word of the Divine to a hammer that shatters a boulder into many pieces: every word that flowed from the Divine mouth, as it were, breaks into the 70 languages of the world.[11] The divine words must be written—but then they must be unwritten, for what are translating or interpreting if not forms of unwriting? Do not be confused: rewriting and unwriting are distinct endeavors. To revise, to rewrite, is to remain wedded to the written word, to linger in its jurisdiction by engaging in a re-crafting of the written words in order to allow them, in their silent countenance, to cut deeper into reality, while simultaneously finding a way to reach off the page into the reader's consciousness. To translate and to interpret—distinct from each other as they may sometimes be—both involve an effort to allow the written word to speak a new language, to speak in new language, which is to say, to speak anew. The Oral Torah is a vast effort of this translation-interpretation kind, cajoling the written words of the Torah out of their state of slumber into the world of the living—and dying—words.

The rabbis were masters of exegesis, and their Torah—the Oral Torah—is, more than anything, their speaking (their voices) through the prism of the written word of the Torah. When Ben Bag Bag says to turn the Torah every which way, again and again, for everything is in it, he is not making a statement about the totality of Torah, its all-inclusiveness.[12] After all, its numbers of letters, words, and sentences are all finite. He is, rather, talking about its infinite possibilities of meaning, the constantly moving horizon which floats above its static text, receding—which is to say progressing—incessantly.

There are, to be sure, rabbinic voices that do indeed understand the finite, written words of Torah as all-inclusive and self-contained. Rabbi Yishmael, commenting on the injunction in the Book of Joshua to never allow the words of Torah to depart from our lips, meditating upon them day and night (Joshua 1:8), concludes—or, to be more precise, ascribes to this verse his view—that we can never study Greek thought, for Torah study must be an all-consuming affair.[13] If the recorded words of the Divine are the only instantiation of the Divine voice ever to have reached the world, then surely we must hold on to them steadfastly, dwelling in them, immersing ourselves in their (still) waters. Rabbi Eliezer understood the finite, recorded words of the Divine as limited, a canteen full of water in an otherwise arid desert. It is no coincidence that Rabbi Eliezer is described by his teacher as a plastered cistern who never lost a drop of the water[14]: he viewed his task as a vessel of Torah to be that of utterly faithful transmission, and certainly not translation, interpretation, innovation, or invention.

This view of the Divine word, however, did not win out—and we know this precisely because it is one out of the many and diverse rabbinic voices that the Oral Torah contains. In their infinite wisdom and their conception of the Divine voice as infinite, the rabbis understood this irony, or perhaps better—tension: one of the legitimate and important interpretations of the Divine voice insists upon its totality, its static nature. For there is a quality of the Divine word that seeks, and, at its best, emulates, perfection and repose. It never fully rests, just like the atoms of a rock never stay still. And yet, it is significant—and, yes, true—to say that the rock is not moving. And so the rabbis understand that the Oral Torah, for the sake of its truth, in order to most accurately and most completely instantiate the infinite nature of the

Written Torah, must contain even those conceptions of the Oral Torah that freeze it in order to hold it in their grasp, even temporarily. The words and verses of the Torah must have 49 facets (which is to say, faces) of purity and, simultaneously, 49 faces of impurity.[15] Later rabbinic literature would posit the Torah to have 70 faces—each one, presumably, facing one of the 70 nations of the world. Like a powerful speaker who addresses a room full of listeners, only to have each and every listener experience that the speaker was addressing her, the Divine voice contains the radical potential to address each and every member of the audience as its unique recipient. God spoke one word, but I heard two, says the Psalmist (Psalms 62:12), a verse that the rabbis seize upon in order to anchor in the Written Torah the ethos of the oracular word that underpins their theological-philosophical-exegetical endeavor.[16]

The spoken word of the Divine rests temporarily in eternal repose as a Written Torah, which, at its outer edge, in its final verses, points to the existence of its own outer edge—and to the jaggedness of that very edge. This, we might say, is the Written Torah's horizon, which, like all horizons, is a place of convergence of the upper and lower realms, more akin to a distorted and blurry continuum than a sharp line. In large part, the rabbinic endeavor was to assume the daunting and holy task of crafting intricately woven ways to ensure an ongoing oscillation between the Written and Oral words. The inseparability of the Written Torah from the Oral Torah implies that their divine and human elements are in constant flux, in an irresolvable tension. To insist, as the rabbis did, upon the continued relevance of both is to view this irresolvability not with suspicion or anger, but rather to embrace it as the defining characteristic of the ongoing relationship between the human and the Divine.

At the most basic level, the rabbis diligently transformed the Written Torah from a pool of stagnant, living waters to an ever-flowing well through the constancy and boundless creativity of their exegesis. But if the Oral Torah consisted merely of an infinitely expanding corpus of exegesis, then the glimpse of infinity that it provided would be nothing more than that offered by any open-ended interpretive community or tradition, be it legal, literary, or philosophical or theological. Rather, what's at stake in the rabbinic conception of Torah that includes both Written and Oral is a once-given and/but ever-expanding, always-in-the-making, constantly revealed, ever-to-be, always-to-come, Torah. The Written Torah, like a spouse, offers a shared past characterized by constancy and fidelity, the truth and the grounding of a shared journey; while the Oral Torah, like a lover, promises an ever-new, not-yet-fully-revealed source of yet-to-be-discovered meaning, fulfillment, and attraction. The rabbis insist that the spouse and the lover can be one and the same.

This always-yet-to-be aspect of the Torah can only be expressed by—because it can only be beckoned by—what Martin Jaffee has called the Torah of the Mouth.[17] Paradoxically, the rabbis touch this infinity by placing their trust in the transience of the Oral tradition. Instead of the infinite precision of black on white, the absolute immutability of the Written word that the scribes offered, the rabbis opted for an oral-performative tradition, which risks being misheard and which transpires in, and over the course of, time. Instead of a Torah written on parchment from an animal carcass, they crafted a Torah embodied in (and by) the sage.[18] This Torah is in his head and mouth, yes, but in the end it is entirely inseparable from him and his wealth of his lived experiences—including the word choice through which he expresses and reveals himself to the outside world. Instead of a recipient who "grasps" the received Word, either with a penetrating gaze or, more receptively, with a hand that holds tight onto the precious gift that he received, insistent upon passing it on—untouched, unsullied, unaffected—to the next generation, the rabbis sought students who heard their masters' words and repeated them verbatim, knowing that the inevitable consequence is that their words would be strung along into an ongoing conversation.[19]

Yet the rabbis were out to transform the Torah, and not just offer an oral addition to the written one. Adding commentary would be, well, an *addition* that merely *commented*, leaving the canonical corpus a corpse. But they sought a new Torah, a transformed Torah consisting of both Written and Oral forms, moments, and instantiations. So they also rematerialized the Written Torah as Spoken Word, insisting that it be read out loud from the open scroll in a community. The absence of vowels and of cantillation marks is not an oversight or a lack, nor is it an invitation for innovation. Rather, it is an essential mechanism for ensuring that at the very moment of lifting the Written word into the realm of sound, a rich, lived tradition—one uncompromising in its insistence on precision—is what enables this transformative moment, which is nothing other than an invitation for the Divine word to enter the communally-shared space. Members of the community—tempted though they may be by eyes that stray, in search of a printed copy of the text—are enjoined to sharpen their ears, to hear the text, to listen attentively for the voices that emerge from the Voiced Written word. We hear "I am God" uttered by a human voice reading from a scroll written by human beings who meticulously transcribed a received written tradition, accompanied by an oral-turned-written tradition of how to vocalize a written text that claims to trace its way back to Moses who heard the Divine word: and we understand, we truly know, their utter inseparability.

That inseparability necessitated, for the rabbis, establishing the revelatory status of the Spoken Torah. They do so in an astounding variety of ways: usually in a subtle fashion, but at times surprisingly open in their subversiveness; their efforts in this regard are as relentless as they are pervasive. Their overarching strategy was to subjugate the Written Torah's meaning—both at the macro- and micro-levels—and indeed its very holiness, to the Oral Torah. "God established a covenant with the people of Israel," claims Rabbi Yoḥanan, "only for the sake of the Oral Torah, as it is written, '... because according to [literally: on the mouth of] these things I established a covenant with you and with Israel' (Exodus 34:27)."[20] This is no subtle defense of the need for modern-day explicators of the Torah's meaning (כי על פי התורה אשר יורו [ki al-pi ha-torah asher yorukha]), nor is it a brazen claim for the Written word's investiture of the rabbis with the sacred authority of the day (יפתח בדורו כשמואל בדורו [Yiftaḥ be-doro ki-Shmuel be-doro]); both those exist elsewhere, and in abundance.[21] What we encounter here is a radical claim regarding the status of the Torah of the Mouth: it is not of *comparable* revelatory status to the Written Torah; it is the very *telos* of the Written Torah. The culmination of the written word that the Divine left behind is none other than the ongoing, divine speaking, as heard by flesh-and-blood rabbis. The Written Torah beckons its unfolding being and becoming within the contours of human existence: that is the ultimate claim of the Oral Torah. The Written Torah as the historicity of our relationship with the Divine—not unlike the past of our human relationships—comprises the grounding of the relationship's present, existing for the sake of the present and the presence, our ongoing relationship with the Divine.[22]

So passionate was Rabbi Yoḥanan's commitment to the orality of the Torah—he did, after all, claim, in contradistinction to Rabbi Elazar, that the majority of the Torah was transmitted orally—that he viewed any effort to write down the spoken Torah as sacrilegious, likening the person who writes down a *halakha* to someone who burns a Torah.[23] Rabbi Yoḥanan compares the two acts, I would suggest, because each seeks to violate the rigid separation between the written and the spoken words, toppling the barrier between gas and solid: the person who writes down the spoken word turns articulated air into solid, ink-on-parchment form, while the person who burns the scroll combusts the written word (back) into gaseous form. For this reason, Reish Lakish, Rabbi Yoḥanan's study partner and nemesis, learned from the verse cited earlier from Exodus (34:27) that an absolute distinction must be maintained between the written and the spoken words: that which is written must stay written, that which is spoken must remain oral. It would seem that their concept of holiness, much like Mary Douglas', requires separation, rigid separation, from the profane.[24]

Indeed, for Rabbi Yoḥanan, as for many of the other rabbis, the Oral Torah offers this temptation. Precisely because of the fact that in its protective shelter Rabbi Yoḥanan converses with the Divine, because it, in all of its vocal urgency, offers a temporality of pure presence so powerful that everything outside of it seems ephemeral and inconsequential, he is tempted to strike his roots only in it, casting aside the rest of the world. This, of course, is the path that Rabbi Shimon bar Yoḥai and his son choose in their desire to stay inside the cave and remain talking heads, buried up to their necks and talking Torah all day long, opting for the eternal life of the present moment (חיי עולם [*hayei olam*]) rather than the transience of this world (חיי שעה [*hayei sha'a*]).[25] But the Oral Torah, as the majority of the sages conceived of it, exists so that it can be lived out in this world—which is to say, it seeks instantiation as halakha. That is, the mystical, other-worldly impulse of *unio mystica*—though clearly voiced within the rabbinic tradition—is overridden by a more vociferous, this-worldly impulse, one that seeks to bring the eternity of the divine word into this very world, where temporality and death reign.[26]

But this dominant voice in rabbinic tradition—the one that insists upon leaving the house of study, thereby risking the forfeiture of eternity in order to give Torah expression in this world—nonetheless fears the grip of temporality. As much as they believe in and advocate the power of the Torah of the Mouth, they fear that their radical and thoroughgoing reconstitution of the-Divine-Word-in-this-world may not succeed in its aspiration to craft a Written–Oral Torah. In order for the Oral Torah to become deed, they reason, it—like the Written Torah—must find an angle of repose. It has to be written down. It is better that one letter of Torah be uprooted than the entirety of Torah be forgotten, reasons Rabbi Yoḥanan.[27] That is, he would uproot the (unwritten) "letter" of the Torah forbidding the act of writing down the spoken word in order to ensure that that Torah of the Mouth achieve the sense of permanence that is reserved for the written word. Not surprisingly, the final flourish of his philosophic-theological move is to frame this claim as exegetical in nature, grounding it in the Written Torah: "It is time to act for the Divine; they have violated [or perhaps:

you should violate] Your Torah" (Psalms 119:126). Once again, the Oral and Written Torahs are woven together indissolubly. In an effort to justify the brazen decision to record the Oral Torah in written form, the rabbinic master who so passionately promotes the oral nature of Torah justifies the decision to instantiate the Oral Torah in written form by finding a verse in which the Written Torah points to its own limits, asserting the occasional need to be violated for the sake of the Divine, whose words it records.

Even once stylized in written form—historians can argue about when exactly that happened—the Oral Torah refuses to enter the straitjacket of the written word. One page of the Talmud, the great work of the Oral tradition, suffices to demonstrate why: the orality of the text is as unmistakable as it is unavoidable. The masterful editing of the Babylonian Talmud is neither about recording conversations that actually took place between the sages nor about constructing conversations that might have taken place in order to create a kind of verbal flow that lends itself to the dialectical reasoning that characterizes Talmudic thought. It is about allowing the spoken word to momentarily dress up as a written one until it can cast that costume aside.

And this written Talmudic word needn't wait long: as soon as its "reader" opens the volume of Talmud, the written word is miraculously and necessarily renewed as spoken word. As my friend, colleague, and teacher Rabbi Mimi Feigelson has said, the difference between a library and a house of study (בית מדרש [beit midrash]) where Talmud is learned is stark: in the library, if there is noise, it is clear that learning is not taking place. The written word jumps from the page directly into the mind of the reader: once the reader has passed the developmentally-early stage of vocalizing the text in order to read it, the vocalization and orality is left behind. She has "advanced" to a higher form of learning: silence.

In the beit midrash, by contrast, silence is a clear indication that learning is not taking place. "Reading" involves two people, face-to-face, with a text between them. The text in its dormant, written form is spoken, brought off the page into the shared actuality and shared space of its two "readers." But these readers are not, in fact, readers. They each vocalize the text and interject their own comments, understandings, associations, interpretations. And they respond to each other. A biblical verse (part of the so-called Written Torah!) is cited by the Talmud, and they go to that chapter of the Bible and read it, commencing a "side" discussion. They return to "the text"—with new understandings: of the Written Torah, of the Talmudic text's appropriation of that verse, of the Talmud itself, of their own evaluation of the Talmudic discussion at hand, of their lives. They jump associatively—either on their own or following the Talmud's lead—to a different Talmudic text, pulling that tome from the shelf, discussing the point-at-hand, related to, but not identical with, the one in their original text of study. Or back and forth to a new theory of property that she has learned about, or an understanding of human agency or intentionality, a learned experience regarding the different roles that nature or society offers to each gender, or a long-forgotten conception of the function of ritual. These strands are woven together—not consciously, intentionally, or artfully, but simply as ongoing, free-associating, open-ended conversation—into a new hour, which is to say, a new chapter, of the Oral Torah.[28] The Oral Torah quite literally continues to become an eternal work in progress, embracing time as its ally rather than a foe that must be overcome. The conversation moves from one of the points at hand to the life of one of the learners, as she shares a disappointment, a job opportunity, a piece of the week's pain, interest in a headline, an intimate detail regarding a relationship: and it is clear that the Oral Torah is not only bound to time; it is bound to life. The Oral Torah is the Living Torah, the Torah of life, תורת חיים [ *Torat ḥayim* ].

This buzz of the *beit midrash*, then, is not merely a learning technique, accessory, or style; it is the very force of life oozing out of every line of the written text, filling the spaces between the letters until the din jumps off the page and fills every empty space in the house of study: it is noisy, raucous, sprawling, unkempt, uncontrolled, uncontrollable, unwieldy, messy, de-centered, chaotic. It is infinite, truly infinite, not just in possibility, but in its reality. The person who seeks totality—or eternity *qua* stillness—will demand a less raucous place.

Ḥoni the Circle-Drawer (How infinitely perfect and self-contained is the shape of the circle!) sought eternity.[29] Walking along the way—isn't that all we do? isn't that what the *halakha* enjoins and enables us to do?—Ḥoni met a man planting a carob tree (it was a carob tree that Rabbi Shimon and his son Rabbi Elazar ate in the cave, withdrawn from the world!). Honi, unable to build a bridge between the present moment and his destination, eternity, could not fathom the sense in such an act. But you will not eat the fruits of your labor, he exclaimed. Unfazed, the man taught Ḥoni—who had such a strong connection to the Master of the Universe that he could bring down rain on demand—that living takes place over time and in time. To participate in life—in the *circle* of life—is to enter a particular world (inhabited by certain carob trees), to partake of them, and to plant others, knowing full well that only the generations to come will see and eat its fruits. Unable to fathom this fully, Ḥoni sat down to do what living people do, to eat, and he did what living people can't help but do—sleep. Only this time his sleep was not 1/60th of death,[30] it was more, as he slept 70 years. He awoke to see the grandson of the planter of the tree enjoying its fruits. And when he went into the house of study, he heard himself quoted, as if he were dead. I'm Ḥoni, he exclaimed. But they paid no heed. The Ḥoni that was living in the lived Oral tradition was more significant, more real—more alive—than this one who was still living. The Ḥoni who walked into the *beit midrash* that day was a dead man walking, for he still did not understand, he could not yet accept, the kind of life that the Torah grants. It is a tree of life for those who accept it—which is to say, for those who accept its partiality, its momentary nature, its orality, its locality.[31] The choice is between a noisy and vibrant oral tradition, a never-ending chain of conversation in which every statement yields an objection, and every answer, another question; and the quiet stillness of the unchanging, eternal word. It is, in the Talmud's admonition, a choice between (the noise of) *ḥevruta* and (the quietude of) death.

To become the spoken word once again, therefore, the Oral Torah does not need a ritualized vocalization of the text in the way that the Written Torah does. It only needs the *beit midrash*, a place where two or more learners gather together to read the text, attack it, be surprised by it, fall in love with it, be outraged by it, identify with it, feel alienated by it, be touched by it: to demand of it, to allow it to demand of them; to bring it into conversation with their lives, to bring their lives into conversation with it. The connection between the learned Torah and life is immediate, urgent, and paramount. The text is spoken and brought here, now. Accrued life is brought into direct contact with the text. And the mediator—to be precise, the mediators—are the learners of the *beit midrash*. But they are not mere mediators. They are the mouths of Torah, of the ongoing Oral Torah, as well as the locus of its revelation.

This learning is no ritual reading of the text: ritualized reading of the Torah requires getting it right, which is to say, approaching the present moment with a clear, already-known understanding of how the text must enter into the shared communal space. The reading must be perfect, and that means that we already possess the standard by which to judge it. This is the demand made of the בעל קורא [*ba'al qore*], the Torah chanter. Studying Torah, by contrast, has no such confidence in itself. It does not know how it must be read, or what it must mean, for it does not know the future: it cannot become ritualized because it does not yet know what it can be, what it may still yet become. This is the deepest truth revealed by the rabbinic notion of—and aspiration for—a חידוש [*hiddush*], a novelty, in the *beit midrash*.

The futurity of the learning of Torah is not the pristine land of a still unexplored, not-yet-conquered piece of knowledge. In fact, learned Torah is not knowledge at all, for it is not, and never can be, possessed in the way that knowledge can. For knowledge is always "grasped": it is at hand and in your hand, and, as such, it is, as Rosenzweig said, of the past.[32] "Future knowledge"—the wide open West that researchers of many disciplines pursue—is nothing more than knowledge of the past that has yet to be discovered. Torah can never be known.

*Wissenschaft des Judentums*, the scientific study of Judaism by contrast, can *only* be known. It is a corpus of knowledge, to be acquired. An enormous gulf separates this study of the cadaver of Judaism from studying Torah. The "objective" study of Judaism—even when its adherents profess their own subjectivity—does just that: it transforms Judaism and its Torah into objects. Here the aspiration is to know what was said. Its glance is always to the past, and its conversation regards what was. The Torah *qua* object of study may be interesting, and it may even find echoes of "relevance" in and for the present; but it can never demand of me, for it remains my object. If it ever becomes my "subject," it is only in the medieval sense of this term: namely, as a vassal submitted to the rule of a sovereign, the reader, who casts her glance its way at will.

To study Torah is to be a conversant, to allow the printed conversation to spill off the page into my lap, to allow its words to enter my mouth, and for me, in turn, to propel these words, its voice, into the *beit midrash*. The Torah is no object out there; it is simultaneously my conversant and the source of the very words—and thus concepts, too—that emerge from my mouth, reflecting my consciousness, all the while shaping it. In this way, as I speak the Oral-turned-Written Torah, it is transformed, miraculously, into Oral Torah anew. The Oral Torah continues to be spoken, first in its language, then in mine, which is to say, it continues to be made. It continues to be revealed.

Open-ended though it may be, Torah study is not contentless. The passion and the discipline of the student of Torah—modeled by Rabbi Shimon bar Yohai who desires two mouths, one to eat and drink with, the other in the holy service of incessant learning of Torah—have roots that go far deeper than intellectual curiosity. They result from, and testify to, the belief—or rather, the deep-down awareness—that every detail matters; that the Divine has yet to be fully revealed; and that every point in reality is an opportunity for manifestation of the Divine. For this reason, the split-end of a hair—for what is a מחלוקת [*maḥloket*] about some picayune aspect of the law if not that?—offers, no less than a wondrous tale regarding Elijah and the sages, an opportunity for the refraction of Divine light. So, too, the most inspiring discussion about moral considerations that arise in the attempt to instantiate the quest for justice in the form of a legal system is, no less than an enigmatic fable regarding harvesting crops through sorcery, such a refraction. Each and every one of these corners of Torah is worthy of its own moment, each warrants a hold on our attention, as we pore through the rabbinic treasure chest, handling its contents delicately. For each and every one of our steps along our path of learning Torah holds the ability to release a divine spark, one that will illuminate our reality, our view of reality, and thus reality itself—in a new light, revealing previously hidden colors and shades. The study of Torah creates the habits of attention that James spoke of, which in turn provide the contour of our experience.

For this reason, the study of Torah also holds the potential to transform our lives entirely—which is to say, us—into something unrecognizable, some apparition of what we knew ourselves to be just moments ago. Strewn in the wake of the Torah I have just learned, my previous self lies mangled, unable to move. Yet learned Torah does not allow for inertness. It is not acquired knowledge that offers a "view" of reality. Rather, it is "knowledge" that necessarily becomes command: it is a call to be transformed, to live differently, to become someone new. The glimpse of infinity that learned Torah offers is not one of hermeneutic possibility; it is one of demand. Each and every aspect of reality can harness or refract divine light, and that means that each and every aspect of my reality demands that my learned Torah receive expression through my actions, in the incessantly pulsating seam between my surroundings and me.

When Rabbi Ḥaninah ben Dosa suggests that anyone whose deeds are greater than his wisdom, his wisdom will endure, he is not dealing in metaphysics.[33] He is dealing in epistemology, suggesting that there is a kind of knowing, a kind of wisdom that is inextricably bound up in the deed. It is a "knowing" that knows truly, that truly knows, only in deed. We may chuckle at the irony of a doctor who smokes, "knowing," as she does, that doing so damages her health. Yet we cannot imagine a student of Torah, or a teacher of Torah—someone who is בן תורה [*ben Torah*], who dwells in Torah, who "knows" a piece of Torah that she does not live out. For this reason, rabbinic literature is replete with examples of learning Torah from the actions of the sages. Their very actions are sources of Torah: they are

Torah-in-deed.[34] In one of the more extreme examples given, we learn of Rabbi Akiva, who follows his teacher, Rabbi Yehoshua, into the restroom in order to know how the Torah demands that we behave in that most private place. Upon hearing this, Ben Azai, Rabbi Akiva's student, expresses his astonishment: how did you dare follow your teacher into the restroom? It's Torah! replies Rabbi Akiva—and I need to learn it! Ben Azai in turn follows Rabbi Akiva into the restroom, and Rabbi Kahana is so bold as to sneak under the bed of his teacher, Rav, to know how he conducts his intimate relations with his wife.[35] In all of these cases, the wisdom and the doing form an inseparable, integrated whole.

Yet the rabbis were not naive, nor were they solipsistic, defining Torah as *however* the sages acted. Examples abound of moral and religious failure on the rabbis' part—and in these moments the rabbis themselves express a heightened awareness of these failures, implicating the authenticity of the Torah they had learned. One of the most famous stories is that of Rabbi Elazar, the son of Rabbi Shimon bar Yoḥai, the exemplar of Torah learning. We are told of a day in which Rabbi Elazar had had his fill of Torah and left the *beit midrash*, traveling alongside a river. דעתה היתה גסה עליו מפני שלמד תורה הרבה [*da'ato hayeta gasa alav mipenei shelamad Torah harbeh*]—his consciousness had become crude and inflated, for he had learned much Torah. He thought that Torah was something he possessed, something to be attained and obtained. He had failed to understand that Torah is living that wisdom out in deed. This piece of Torah, or meta-Torah, he had yet to learn. Along the way (again, he is on the way!) he encounters an unsightly person—the text tells us that he was indeed "ugly"—and Rabbi Elazar asks him if all of the inhabitants of his town were as ugly as he. I don't know, the man replies, go and ask the artisan who made me. Rabbi Elazar then understands that he has sinned, so he dismounts his horse, an act of humility showing simultaneously that he failed in Torah, and that this person, at least momentarily, is his teacher of Torah. Forgive me, he says. The man refuses at first, until finally, as they approach the nearby town, residents of the town emerge to greet Rabbi Elazar, "great" as he is in Torah. Forgive him, plead the residents, for he is a master of Torah. We the readers know that these town folk have not the slightest clue of what greatness in Torah is, for we understand that one cannot be a master of Torah without being great in deed. If this is your rabbi, exclaims the man, there should be as few as possible like him in Israel.

The Torah's learners do not always succeed in transforming it into deed. In silent patience, the Torah lingers, enduring the failures and foibles of its flawed keepers. Like the prophetic sting that continues to rankle well beyond its failure to effectuate political change, the learned Torah—even when it is not lived out as deed—continues to wield impact.[36] For this reason, the *Sefat Emet* says that while a transgression nullifies a *mitzvah*, it cannot nullify learned Torah.[37] Elisha's lived life continues to play itself out in conversation with Torah, and in its language and concepts, even as he rebels against it. Despite our failure of deed and the concomitant collapse of "wisdom," the Torah's demand is unremittent: like its written words that wait to be spoken, learned Torah waits to be lived.

Halakha is this very moment of assent on our part: an endless effort to express holiness in every crevice of our lives. Learned Torah demands realization, which means a willingness to forego the comfort of hermeneutic possibility and step into the finite, limited realm of actuality. Comfort and self-satisfaction are the rarest of commodities in this sphere, for just beneath the crest of nearly every action lurks a nagging and gnawing awareness that it could have been otherwise; that the infinity of the divine command could not receive full expression in this finite world; that there was truth in the action I chose not. Halakha is Torah as expressed in action, informed by an awareness of its own partial nature. Halakha is the infinite divine word of Torah as expressed in the discrete, hard, finite realm of doing.

Doing is not saying, nor is it learning. Saying, writing, learning: these are all forms of doing, but doing is beyond them.

I utter the words "I love you." In them and through them I offer a part of me to my friend or lover, revealing myself. Speaking those words in the privacy of our home offers one horizon of possibility. But I may decide to utter those words in the shared public space of a coffeehouse, and the action of relocating that private speaking into a public space alters the saying. The spoken words—though identical—are different forms of action. I could also utter those words under a marriage canopy, opening up our shared space of intimacy to our invited guests, again transforming the speaking into yet a different form of action. I could write those words down, in an intimate letter or perhaps even in a public declaration of my love, seeking to grant my words the kind of permanence and weight that only the written word encapsulates. In each of these cases, the allegedly transparent words are expressed in and as a different form of doing. The vessels of action in which we place these words—speech, writing, public speech, private speech, private speech in a public place, a text message, a post on Facebook, an intimate letter—each crafts a unique meaning out of these same words, thus instantiating not only the malleability of the meaning of language, but also the extent to which every verbal expression is a discrete form of action.

But I may also fall silent, sensing the presence of my friend or beloved—living, acting, and being in this presence, bound to her through shared action. We may walk in silence; view an object or a movie; work alongside each other. In all of these cases, we are bound—in time, in our doing. A deceptively profound intimacy hides in the silence of this shared action, which is why we often feel so uncomfortable in the silent presence of someone with whom we do not share intimacy. In these moments, if we choose to be present with and toward the other person, we are thrust into direct contact with her being—with her. That presence can be overwhelming, in much the same way that the direct, untempered gaze into another's eyes can prove so powerful that we must, within seconds, avert our gaze, even momentarily. Terrified by the demand of this intimacy, we often fill the space between us with words; only in this instance the words do not serve as a bridge between us, revealing our inner depths to the other across the gulf separating us. For, in this case, between us there lies not a void but a (silent but) genuine connection, and so the words now come to displace this intimacy. Not saying is also doing.

Halakha asserts the possibility of—and insists upon—the shared language of action. That is, it is not only, as described earlier, an incessant, unmitigated, uncompromising, aspirational command to realize holiness to the greatest extent possible in every place and moment. It is also a demand that this spiritual striving be fundamentally interpersonal in nature. Holiness, to the extent that it will be realized, is—and must be—a communal endeavor.

Although speech, revelatory speech, constitutes connective tissue between human beings, the halakhic community is not bound by speech. Members of the community do not speak halakha: they may speak Torah, and, if their "profane" speech is spoken with appropriate sensitivity and mindfulness, they may speak halakhically. Rather, the community is halakhic in, by, and through its norms of shared praxis: through its doing. The community is bound and constituted neither by language nor by belief. In their doing—their shared, speechless acts—individuals of varying theology, outlook, style, and temperament establish communal space, which is to say, community.

## Notes

1. See, for example, Yisrael Hopstein (The Maggid of Kozhnitz), *Avodat Yisrael* on *Shulkhan Aruh*, Oreḥ Ḥayim 433 3 [Hebrew].

2. Franz Rosenzweig, "The New Thinking," in *Franz Rosenzweig's 'The New Thinking'*, ed. and trans. Alan Udoff and Barbara E. Galli (New York: Syracuse, 1999), 81–84. See also Rosenzweig, *Star of Redemption*, 295–296 and Rosenzweig, *Understanding the Sick and the Healthy*, 71–74.

3. B.T. Sanhedrin 90b.

4. See Hartman, *A Living Covenant*, pp. 6–8. See also Yeshayahu Leibowitz, "The Holiness of the Holy Scriptures," in Leibowitz, *Judaism, The Jewish People, and the State of Israel*, 346–350 [Hebrew]. For an English gloss on this, see "Ahistorical Thinkers in Judaism" in Leibowitz, *Judaism, Human Values, and the Jewish State*, 96–105.

5. "There is a very serious traditional orientation to the covenant that points in the direction opposite to the one that I am suggesting in this work. . . . This orientation claims that the closer one is to Sinai, the more truly one can understand the meaning of Torah and live authentically with God. The further one gets away from Sinai, the more one must be obedient and reverential to those earlier generations, who mediate in a more authentic way the living word of Torah. From this perspective, the present can find legitimacy only through the authentication of the past" (Hartman, *A Living Covenant*, 11). See also Hartman, *The God Who Hates Lies*, 15–16.

6. Exodus 19–20, esp. 20:14.

7. B.T. Kiddushin 39a.

8. Jorge Luis Borges, "Funes, the Memorious," in Jorge Luis Borges, *Ficciones*, translated by Emecé Editores (New York: Grove Press, 1962).

9. Hayyim Nachman Bialik, "Language Closing and Disclosing," trans. Yael Lotan, in *The Heart and the Fountain: An Anthology of Jewish Mystical Experiences*, ed. Joseph Dan (New York: Oxford University Press, 2003), 261.

10. J.T. Berachot 1:2.

11. "The school of Rabbi Yishmael taught . . . [j]ust as a hammer breaks a stone into several fragments, so too, each and every utterance that emerged from the mouth of the Blessed Holy One divided into seventy languages" (B.T. Shabbat 88b).

12. Mishna Avot 5:22.

13. "Ben Damah, son of Rabbi Yishmael's sister, asked Rabbi Yishmael: 'One such as I, who has studied all of the Torah, what is the law with regard to my studying Greek wisdom?' Rabbi Yishmael recited this verse: '"This book of Torah shall not depart from your mouth; rather you shall contemplate it day and night" (Joshua 1:8). Go out and find a moment that is neither the day nor the night, and study in it Greek wisdom!'" (B.T. Menahot 99b).

14. Mishna Avot 2:8.

15. See *Midrash Tehillim* on Psalms 12:7. For a concise summary of how the 49 faces of Torah became 70, see Hananel Mack's article "The Seventy Faces

of the Torah: Tracing the Development of a Phrase" [Hebrew], available at http://mikranet.cet.ac.il/pages/item.asp?item=18290

16. See *Mekhilta of Rabbi Yishmael*, Parashat Beshalaḥ, Parasha 8; see also B.T. Shabbbat 88b on Jeremiah 23:29.

17. "The point, however, is that the tradition surviving among the Sages [was] transmitted in the original way—by patient repetition, from master to disciple, from mouth to ear, and from ear to memory, without the intervention of a written text. This teaching is thoroughly oral; in the parlance of the Talmud and other early rabbinic writings, it is Oral Torah or, as I prefer to render it— Torah in the Mouth" Martin Jaffee, *Torah in the Mouth* (New York: Oxford University Press, 2001), 5.

18. Haninah Ben-Menahem, 'Two Talmudic Understandings of the Dictum "Appoint for Yourself a Teacher"', in *Thinking Impossibilities: The Intellectual Legacy of Amos Funkenstein*, ed. R.S. Westman and D. Biale, (Toronto: University of Toronto Press), 2008.

19. I have spoken of "he" rather than "she" in this paragraph because I am describing the rabbis' endeavor.

20. B.T. Gittin 60b.

21. See, for example, the rabbinic treatment of the Biblical verse, "You shall go according to the Torah that they will instruct you … veering neither right nor left" (Deuteronomy 17:11). Among others, see Rashi's and Nachmanides' commentaries on Deuteronomy 17:11; *Song of Songs Rabba* Parasha A; *Sifre Devarim* 154; and J.T. Horayot 1:1. See also the phrase "Yiftah in his generation is akin to Shmuel in his generation" (B.T. Rosh Hashanah 25b).

22. Rosenzweig, *Star of Redemption*, 183–184.

23. B.T. Temurah 14b.

24. Mary Douglas, *Purity and Danger: An Analysis of the Concepts of Pollution and Taboo* (New York: Ark, 1988).

25. B.T. Shabbat 33b.

26. For two of the better known instances (among many), see the story of Rabbi Shimon bar Yoḥai who withdraws into a cave with his son (B.T. Shabbat 33b), or the description of how Rabbi Akiva would engage in ecstatic prayer when alone (B.T. Brakhot 31a).

27. B.T. Temura 14b. See also B.T. Gittin 60a.

28. For further discussion of the nature of learning in the Beit Midrash, see Elie Holzer with Orit Kent, *A Philosophy of Havruta: Understanding and Teaching the Art of Text Study in Pairs* (Boston: Academic Studies Press, 2013).

29. B.T. Taanit 23b, Shabbat 33b.

30. B.T. Brakhot 57b.

31. "It is a tree of life to all who grasp it, and whoever holds on to it is happy; its ways are ways of pleasantness, and all it paths are peace" (Proverbs 3:17–18).

This verse is integrated into the *siddur* at the time that the Torah scroll is returned to the ark.

32. Rosenzweig, *Star of Redemption*, 132–133.

33. Avot 3:9.

34. Ben-Menahem, "Two Talmudic Understandings."

35. B.T. Brakhot 62a.

36. Martin Buber, *Israel and the World*, (Syracuse: Syracuse University Press, 1997), 112. See also Ahad Ha-'Am, "Priest and Prophet," in *Selected Essays of Ahad Ha-'Am*, trans. and ed. Leon Simon (New York: Atheneum, 1981).

37. Yehuda Aryeh Leib Alter of Gur, *Sefat Emet*, Parashat Tzav, 1871 [Hebrew].

# CHAPTER 3

# Shared Spacetime: Community

**Abstract** In this chapter, Wiener Dow explores the way in which individuals—by sharing in time, and, to a lesser extent, space—form community through deed. The halakha thus weds together two areas of the ineffable, communal existence and theological truth, and this understanding renders intelligible key concepts of the halakha. *Kiddush Ha-shem*, the sanctification of the divine name, lies at the heart of Jewish law because it places paramount import upon the way in which the external observer views the individual's act. *Maḥloket*, disagreement, is central to halakha because it allows for divergent understandings of the divine command. The charge of the halakha as communal religious praxis results from the oscillation between inwardness that characterizes the encounter with the Divine and an uncompromising demand of the intersubjectivity of the deed.

**Keywords** halakha and community • Jewish communal norm • *Kiddush Ha-shem* • *Marit Ayin* • *Mipenei darkei shalom*/the ways of peace • *Maḥloket*/disagreement

## ACTION AND THE CONSTITUTION OF COMMUNITY

Ernst Akiva Simon allegedly once quipped, "I cannot speak with the people with whom I pray, and the people with whom I can speak do not pray." Simon's observation is not, fundamentally, a testament to his odd matrix of friends. Rather, it is reflective of the fundamental difference between speech

© The Author(s) 2017
L. Wiener Dow, *The Going*,
https://doi.org/10.1007/978-3-319-68831-2_3

and prayer. Prayer—at least in its Jewish variant—tends to be laden heavily with words, frequently performed and understood as a kind of speech to or at the Divine; for this reason, it is often mistaken as a mode of speech. Yet it is most certainly not speech. Anyone who has tried to engage in prayer while two people in close proximity converse can attest to this fact. In a different situation—say, while I sit at a table in a café and talk with someone else, or even while I sit in solitude in a library trying to read—such a conversation, while distracting, would never render the kind of devastation that it does to the possibility of prayer. For what's at stake in someone's speaking during our act of prayer is not my ability to concentrate on my doings, be it conversation or thought. Rather, in and with their speech, my neighbors disavow themselves of the communal endeavor of prayer. Aware of the distinction between the act of speech and the act of prayer, Simon was thus noting (and perhaps lamenting) the discontinuity between his two experiences: the people with whom, as individuals, he could share in discourse did not coincide with those with whom he could participate in the act of prayer.

Here we arrive at a second point that we can tease out of Simon's utterance: speech establishes interpersonal relationship, but only action (such as prayer) can establish community. A group of people cannot speak qua community; in fact, the din of multiple people speaking simultaneously is, more often than not, a force of division. What they can do together is—to do. To listen, to build, to observe, to disregard, to clap, to sing, to pray. It is precisely this shared doing—not ideology, not belief, and not locale—that constitutes community.

That a community is not bound by location seems self-evident to us in this day of "virtual" and "imagined" communities. Modernity and postmodernity have altered our sense of community so fundamentally and so irrevocably that we must work especially hard in order to take seriously the halakha's claim that the predominant danger we face is in underestimating the import of real, genuine, human interaction in the life of community. And yet a tandem danger exists: we may, in our effort to combat the flimsiness and superficiality of virtual and imagined communities, argue that community necessarily requires geographical circumscription. To be sure, there is truth in this critique of models of mobile communities of all sorts. For them, as for individuals in relationship, geographic distance can impose a serious impediment to their essential cohesiveness, especially over time. Moreover, certain aspects of organic communal life will remain inaccessible absent of shared physical space. But geographical proximity is not constitutive of community.

Neither are ideology and belief, as I mentioned previously. That is not to say that they are unimportant in shaping community. A community's elite—its leaders, its educators, its artists, its intelligentsia—craft ideas, embrace concepts, and articulate beliefs that will trickle their way into broader discourse, in turn impacting the beliefs and commitments of the community's members. But ultimately this process of integration and internalization is done by individuals as individuals, and so they cannot become community by virtue of this process. Rather, the moment of weight, the point at which they become community, is in the outward expression of these ideas—for that outward expression necessarily transpires in the interstices between the individual and her surrounding world, whether that space be intimate, quasi-public, or fully public.

To be sure, nomos is always tied to narrative. Long before Robert Cover argued for their interdependence, the rabbis had woven halakha and aggadah, law and narrative, into a tightly knit fabric.[1] But nomos is not emergent from or subject to narrative. The two flow from one another and back to each other unceasingly. And so, while community is inconceivable absent of sustaining narratives, it comes into being in the moment of action—and is sustained, nourished, and regenerated through the discrete actions themselves.

The kibbutz movement in Israel failed to offer a sustainable model of Jewish community because its leaders tried to establish and cultivate community principally through ideology, underestimating the import of the weave of law, custom, and living that animate the daily life of a community. Patterns of living were so beholden to the ideology that, once the ideology suffered major blows, the life force of the communities endured a total collapse. Though he was not a member of a kibbutz, Ḥayyim Nahman Bialik, the great poet and a key figure in the Second Aliyah, understood that the secular Zionist movement needed a halakha, a praxis through which to be constituted.[2] Sociologists of American Jewry "discovered" the same thing when they found that the three activities that are by far the likeliest to result in the Jewish commitment of the child are day school, Jewish summer camps, and trips to Israel.[3] What all three share in common—especially the latter two—is their immersing the child in a thoroughgoing framework of doing in which every sphere of action and interaction takes place in the context of Jewish community.

נעשה ונשמע [ *Na'aseh ve-nishma*], we will do and we will hear. Rosenzweig is right to say that this phrase conveys the primacy of the act, hinting further that our hearing, our understanding, is secondary both in sequence and in importance. We hear differently, he correctly points out, when we hear in the doing.[4] But Rosenzweig's gloss fails to capture a vital aspect of *na'aseh ve-nishma*: the utterance of the children of Israel at Sinai—and yes, it is of significance that the Torah is revealed to all of the people as a people—is a communal utterance, and it is in the plural. That is, *na'aseh ve-nishma* is not, first and foremost, a manifesto of existential philosophy. It is a statement of the deepest ethos of the Jewish community: We will do. And we begin our doing by saying that we will do. The doing is definitive of the community, and halakha is that doing. Halakha cannot speak; it can only do, and so my attempt in this chapter to give it a voice is an attempt to dress it in an outfit that is too small.

## TEASING APART COMMUNITY, COMMUNAL NORM, AND COMMUNAL ACTION

And yet, despite the way in which a community defines itself in its doing, the two never conflate fully. The community and the communal norm can be teased apart. An element of communal belonging can consist of the communal norm that I (or we) do not observe. A different form of observance—or even non-observance—can comprise a form of observance.

The halakha is the normative life of the Jewish community, but the two entities are not coterminous. As we shall see when we examine the subject of maḥloket, the halakhic system can withstand diversity in the realm of opinion, and, to an astounding degree, even when it spills over into the realm of praxis. In fact, maḥloket serves as a connecting wedge. On the one hand, it divides the community, fracturing it into splinter groups. On the other hand, it serves as a bridge that traverses the chasm that separates the communities.

Yet, in one well-known incident, Rabban Gamliel asserts with crude force the limits of halakhic flexibility, as determined by the limits of maḥloket to bridge the ravine of practice separating two communities. In this incident, Rabban Gamliel, the President, and Rabbi Yehoshua disagree about what constitutes valid testimony for the new moon.[5] This disagreement, in turn, spurs a fundamental disagreement regarding the fixing of the calendar, and Rabban Gamliel, known for his authoritarian nature, pulls rank. He issues an edict to Rabbi Yehoshua that he must take his cane and coins and travel to see him on the day that is, according to Rabbi Yehoshua's calculations, Yom Kippur. Rabbi Yehoshua, in great consternation, consults Rabbi Akiva and Rabbi Dosa Ben Horcanus, both of whom tell him that he must do as Rabban Gamliel demands. Rabbi Yehoshua does so, and, as he enters, Rabban Gamliel stands—a gesture of respect issued by someone of lower status to someone of higher status—and kisses Rabbi Yehoshua on the forehead, an indication of affection from someone of higher status to someone of lower status, proclaiming, "Come in peace, my teacher and my student. My teacher in wisdom, my student in accepting my decree."

What at first glance may appear in this story to be a demand for conformity in behavior constitutes only the surface of a discussion whose depths touch upon the way in which place and time define community. In essence, Rabban Gamliel is arguing that the cohesiveness of the halakhic community can overcome geographical distance—but only on the condition that the community shares time. That is why he must force the hand of Rabbi Yehoshua, who calculates the calendar differently. Even if we share the same space, Rabban Gamliel says, that is insufficient for us to participate in shared communal life: we must meet in time.

## Shared Time

What does it mean for human beings to meet in time? Ultimately, it implies that individuals relinquish a part of their autonomy in order to share their doing with others in time. "My" time becomes "our" time. We are wont to do that precisely because of the depth of the impingement upon our autonomy. We prefer to send an email or text message, or to leave a voicemail, rather than to speak to the person over the phone, for in the former instances we remain in full control of our time. When we meet someone in time we choose to forego some portion of our independence. It is an act of heteronomy, the sine qua non of community.

This decision is a momentous one precisely because of the import—existential and philosophical—of "my time." For what is "my time" if not my borrowed time, that thing I stake my very existence on, the thing that's most truly mine even if it's not truly mine, as I live in the valley of the shadow of my death while it draws inexorably near? For even if I don't know when it will come, I know this with certainty: with every passing instant it has come closer. Thus, to participate in the life—which is to say, the time—of community is to stake my life in that of the community. I trade in a portion of my temporality for the flash of eternity that the community promises. The glimmer in the eye of the grandparent present at her grandchild's entry into the community is the refraction of the light of eternity: in that moment, she is taken to the precipice of her lived years and offered a glimpse of the life that goes on, the pulsating wave of life which continues forward, even as she recedes from its crest.

## HALAKHA: SHARED DOING IN THE SPACETIME MANIFOLD

At this point, we can formulate an interim definition of the halakha: the Jewish communities' shared—but not identical—doing in time. Rooted in and emergent from the learned conversation of Torah, it is an aspirational doing that seeks to infuse every crevice of our momentary, this-worldly existence with significance. And because every piece of existence can refract divine light, every interaction—indeed, every action, even the most private ones—holds open the promise of expressing holiness. The fundamentally communal nature of this aspiration implies that communal life in all of its manifestations can be an avenue of expression for this aspiration. In this way, the community's dual pull of shared space and shared time becomes an opportunity—nay, an obligation—for instantiating holiness and eternity in this world.

Against the backdrop of this understanding of the halakha, it becomes clear why prayer so often—even if unnecessarily—occupies a central place in attempts to understand the halakha. Heschel could call mitzvot "prayer as deed" precisely because the multilayeredness of prayer offers a profound cross section of the halakhic moment.[6] The event of prayer brings to the fore not only the undeniable centrality of theology to the halakhic system, in addition to the poles of קבע וכוונה [keva and kavana]—fixed structure and intentionality. More important to the context of our discussion, prayer demands the individual's very innermost—the deepest, hardly-effable recesses of her soul—all the while insisting that the she sacrifice some of her particularity in order to participate in a larger communal endeavor. When those two forces come together into one fabric—be it hesitatingly or enthusiastically, awkwardly or gracefully—the individual constituent strands are never effaced. Then—and only then—may the individuals and the community, separately and together, utter those privileged words that the halakhic tradition limits to דבר שבקדושה [davar she-bikdusha], a matter of holiness.

If the halakha is shared doing in time, then—given the impossibility of separating space and time from the unified manifold that they comprise— we must acknowledge the halakhic community's spatial dimension. The rabbis crafted a calendar that enabled Jews outside of the Land of Israel to participate in the shared time of the Jewish community, overcoming phys- ical distance. In so doing, they posit the supra-territorial nature of the halakhic community. Yet, we know well from our attempts to bridge physical distance through the myriad of mechanisms that technology has put at our disposal, a person on the screen or on the phone can be there for us—but never here with us. The full depth of human existence requires presence in all of its rich connotation.

## SHABBAT AND THE DEMARCATION OF HALAKHIC COMMUNITY

The centerpiece of the halakhic life is, no doubt, Shabbat, for it is all about this unfettered, uncompromised presence—in time and in place. Heschel wrote a beautiful and powerful meditation on Shabbat as a palace in time, and his descriptions of Shabbat's ability to bring eternity into time are as accurate as they are profound.[7] Yet *The Sabbath* fails to capture the intricate weave between time and place that Shabbat entails. The very first Mishnah in the tractate of Shabbat portends one of the principle themes of the whole tractate: an unrelenting attempt to cast a contour of space that gradually extends the private space of the individual into a blurred continuum with the shared space of the community.[8] These extended lines continue in one fashion or another—regulating the ability to move physical objects from one place to another—until they reach תחום שבת [*tehum Shabbat*] "the area of Shabbat," the geographical area beyond which a person may not walk on Shabbat (approximately 1 km from the outer boundary of the community). Bound to her community on Shabbat, the individual may nonetheless extend her own "Shabbat area" in one direction beyond the 1 km limita- tion, but with each extension in that direction she must limit herself in the opposite direction. The result of this complex nexus of laws is that the 25 hours of Sabbath—for what is the Sabbath if not a piece of time, carved out from time's continuum—do more than align the individual with the rhythm of cosmic time, forcing her to cede all pretense that she can be master of anything, even her own time. They also bind her to a physical space—and to the community of individuals who inhabit that space during those hours.[9]

The story is told, in different variations, of the rabbi-turned-apostate, Elisha ben Abuya, who rode on his horse through the Jewish community on Shabbat, thus violating Shabbat publicly. At that time, Rabbi Meir—his student, a sage so prominent and so dominant that it is said that the anonymous voice of the Mishna is his and that, further, whenever the sages of the Mishna determined that the halakha was not according to his position, it was only because they failed to understand the depth of this thought[10]—is poised in the house of study, offering his weekly homily. Rabbi Meir's students rush in to tell him that "his rabbi" is passing by, and Rabbi Meir stops mid-sentence and dashes outside to greet his teacher and to speak words of Torah with him. (Can you imagine a teacher of such enormous stature doing this?) Their exchange—fascinating and edifying as it is—is eclipsed only by its abrupt conclusion. You must turn around, Elisha says to Rabbi Meir. Why?, asks Rabbi Meir. Because I've counted my horse's footsteps, and so I know that we've now reached (what is for you) the area of Shabbat. Rabbi Meir enjoins, if you know so much Torah, how can you not live out that Torah in deed?! Return! —by which Rabbi Meir means, return to the normative fold of the community. Elisha responds that, existentially speaking, he cannot do so.

The story—even in the skeletal version I have offered—is rich beyond our ability to exhaust here, touching upon questions of the relationship between study and lived ideas; the nature of human freedom; teacher–student relationships; and the possibilities, and limits, of pluralism in Torah study and in halakhic praxis. It is this last point that is relevant for our present discussion: namely, the import of Rabbi Meir and Elisha's arrival at the border of the Shabbat area. Up until that point, they could talk Torah together, an intimate hevruta, two learners in dialog—perhaps playful, perhaps aggressive—engaging in the spoken word. Yet this is a camaraderie and intimacy of two—sharing Torah and sharing a journey walking together. But they are unable to share in the life of the same community, which is why Rabbi Meir, upon reaching the border of the area of Shabbat, must turn around, even while Elisha—sensitive though he may be regarding Rabbi Meir's needs and observances—rides on. He, for his own sake, cannot turn back: he is not a part of the community that binds—and limits—Rabbi Meir. Rabbi Meir, for his part, mourns—ostensibly for Elisha, whom he fears will be punished for his apostasy. But the reader senses that, in fact, Rabbi Meir is mourning the poverty of the community that cannot contain Elisha in its midst. They are not part of the same lived community, and it is that border of the area of Shabbat, where space and time join in a delicate weave to bind individuals into shared fabric of action, that testifies to the gulf that separates them.

In this story, the border at which Rabbi Meir and Elisha part ways demarcates not only the area of Shabbat that confines and defines that specific geographic halakhic community, but the halakhic community in its broadest sense. Indeed, though we have spoken thus far about shared communal action in the ritual spheres of prayer and Shabbat, the halakha claims relevance in every sphere of a person's lived life, so surely the borders of the halakhic community must include in their midst arenas of action far more variegated than those associated with ritual behavior. Business dealings; attitudes toward parents, children, and elders; distributive justice, social justice, and treatment of disadvantaged; care for the environment and the physical world; the composition and integrity of family units; intimate relations; matters of equity; relations between neighbors; the ordering of everyday social intercourse: surely these must all define the halakhic community, with border markers no less distinct than the 2000 אמה [amah] which define the "ins" and "outs" of the Shabbat borders of the community. Yet also, issues not overtly ethical in nature—sexual mores; conventions and uses of language and speech; attitudes toward body and physicality; our consumption of food and drink; choices about how to spend our time and what content with which to fill our days, our eyes, and our souls—all of these are matters of halakha not merely because they offer opportunities for lived-out Torah, encapsulating our aspirations for holiness in our daily actions. They are halakha because, without exception, they all— even the ones that take place in spaces of intimacy and privacy—draw from, express, and contribute to communal norm.

## WEAVING TOGETHER COMMUNAL ACTION AND COMMUNAL NORM

This is not to say, of course, that every action conforms to the existent halakhic communal norm; only that it is bound, in some ineluctable way, to the amalgamated sum of communal activity, which in turn exerts a profound, if often silent, impact on the ongoing evolution of the norm. Aware of this dynamic interplay between nomos and the community, a rabbinic dictum disqualifies any enactment that the majority of the public will be unable to uphold.[11] This is not merely a strategy for effective governance: it expresses a deep understanding that, as the legend goes, the Torah was not given to heavenly angels[12]: it was given to people, and the cumulative effect of disobedience of the law is profoundly inimical, unraveling the communal norm, and, with it, the community itself.[13]

How else can we understand the advice of Rabbi Ullah to the person who has, to borrow from Nathan Englander, an unbearable urge that he must relieve?[14] Rabbi Ullah suggests that the person overcome by his desire to sin—presumably sexually—go someplace where no one knows him, don black clothes, cover himself in black, and do as his heart desires, rather than desecrating the divine name publicly.[15] Surely Rabbi Ullah's preference is that this person refrains from the deplorable action: the thoroughgoing nature of the command of holiness cannot apportion areas of action that are irrelevant or even insignificant.[16] Yet, in the greatest rabbinic fashion, Rabbi Ullah knows how and when to recede in the face of human frailty—to be a priest and not a prophet, to use Ahad Ha-'Am's distinction.[17] And yet, he also understands that every single action and every single inaction, every deed and every misdeed, contributes to—or gnaws away at—the communal norm. The public desecration of the divine name about which Rabbi Ullah is concerned is nothing other than the impugning of the One who commands.

### THE OCULAR CONSTITUTION OF COMMUNITY: קידוש ה' [KIDDUSH HASHEM] AND מראית עין [MAR'IT AYIN]

Here Rabbi Ullah follows the well-trodden (and stunningly beautiful!) path of sages who inquired as to the idea of consecrating the divine name.[18] The discussion begins modestly, with sages staking out the definition of the converse—namely, what constitutes desecration of the divine name. In my lived life, enjoins Rav, purchasing meat without paying immediately entails a desecration of the divine name. As the Talmudic discourse continues, other mundane examples abound from the lives of sages. Disparate though they are, the various actions share an unmistakable commonality: the reaction they provoke in onlookers. Basing himself upon the discussion of earlier Tanaitic sages, Abaye unsettles the reader by clarifying that ultimately the subject under discussion is the deepest question that a Jew who aspires to live halakhically must face: how do I love the Divine?

Even more startling than the clarity and challenge of the question that Abaye has posed is the convoluted, decentered answer that he proposes. To love the Divine, suggests Abaye, is to act in a way that causes others, who observe my actions, to love the divine name. That transpires, continues the

Talmud, when a person's actions serve as a source of admiration and inspiration for the people observing her. The onlooker exclaims: "Happy are that person's parents and rabbi who taught her Torah! Just look at [how] beautiful her behavior is!" Articulated as a positive theological position, Abaye's claim goes as follows: I love the Divine by acting and interacting in ways that people admire. How people perceive my behavior is a force so palpable and substantial that it is tantamount to—nay, identical with—loving the Divine.

Here we see the way in which the halakha weaves together two strands of the ineffable. It is not merely that words are inadequate to express the command to love the Divine, and words also happen to prove insufficient in creating the intersubjective space in which and through which community forms. Rather, the halakha reveals the way in which these two aspects of the ineffable are profoundly linked. Service of the Divine must receive outward expression in action, and this action necessarily reverberates in that expanse that lies beyond the individual. It is in that shared space of action that community is wordlessly constituted. Holy deed is inextricably communal, and communal action cannot disavow itself of its spiritual valence.

*Kiddush Ha-shem*, the sanctification of the divine name, pulsates at the heart of the entire halakhic endeavor, for every action or inaction on the individual's part must answer to this ultimate and uncompromising standard. Does my action—were it to be known—sanctify the divine name? The question the halakha poses to the individual is not Kant's regarding the universalizability of the action.[19] Rather, the individual is coaxed into inviting the watchful eyes of the community into the recesses of her private sphere. "And I shall be sanctified amongst you" (Leviticus 22:32), says the Divine. The verse goes on to add that the Divine makes Israel holy ("I am YHWH who makes you holy")—but the rabbis of the Talmud ignore that part of the verse, for their concept of holiness doesn't lend itself to claims of ontology regarding the community.[20] In their estimation, it is not the Divine that bestows holiness unto the community; rather, it is the community that sanctifies the Divine through deed, by acting in a way that observers—both inside and outside of the community—deem worthy of admiration and emulation.

But the halakha reveals the Divine and the community to share in more than the ineffable realm of action; they are also partners in casting a glance—and with it a form of judgment—at the individual. You shall be mindful of the One before Whom you stand, enjoins the Mishnah in Avot in two variants (2:1 and 3:1). It is a failure of the religious imagination, my ḥevruta, Rabbi Joel Levy once wrote, not to walk with a constant awareness of the Divine observing our each and every action. Indeed, one could rightfully understand Yom Kippur as a colossal effort on the part of the rabbis to fashion a day—and, in the days of repentance, a period of the year—during which we succeed at this enterprise of envisioning the watchful eye of the Divine. Through the category of sanctification (or desecration) of the divine name, the halakha bestows upon every act the potential to become of theological moment. That is the true and full meaning of the internalized glance of the Divine.

But where our religious imagination may fail us, the awesome power of the communal glance surely will not. This is likely the reason that Yom Kippur, in its ritual and its liturgy, is understood as a communal process of expiation, despite its supremely existential import for the individual. Even absent the powerful and pernicious effect of the possibility of others' talking about us, the mere facticity of the glance—or, to be even more precise, the possibility of the glance—is sufficient to leave us altered, fearful of the judgment, conscious and self-critical of our deed and even our demeanor.

We can best understand what the halakha is after by contrasting it with Kant's categorical imperative.[21] Kant's noble offering is of a universal criterion of judgment that applies to any and every course of behavior. The moral character of an action is determined precisely by the universalizability of its application: what if everyone were to behave this way? By contrast, the halakha posits the consideration of *Mar'it Ayin*, a test of behavior equally rigorous, but radically different in nature. I must ask myself: What will observers of my behavior think about it? The force of the questions arises not from its universal nature but from its particularity: certain people will observe a particular action of mine and arrive at a certain conclusion: here is a standard rooted deeply in local knowledge and nomos, one that must take into account a particular point of view—the line of sight of the observer. What is determinate is not my intention (as Kant would have it), nor even my action itself. Instead, the reality of my behavior in its social context assumes palpable significance. With *Mar'it Ayin*, the internalized glance of the other—and not just any other, but particular others—becomes a cornerstone of the halakha.

## The Internalized Glance

The impact of this internalized glance is profound: the self becomes decentered, for each and every action is subject to external scrutiny. In fact, the Babylonian Talmud sides with Rav, who goes so far as to hold that any action that would be forbidden publicly because of *Mar'it Ayin* is forbidden even in the innermost chambers.[22] And so a complex dialectic ensues in the halakha between *Mar'it Ayin* and *Kiddush Ha-shem*, once we understand their far-reaching powers and the complex nexus of interaction between them. The former moment of decision stems from a consideration of an outwardness spawned by the communal glance and my attentiveness to it. The latter moment, by contrast, thrusts my every action and being into the countenance of divine light. To be sure, as we saw earlier, this desire to sanctify the divine name occurs against a public backdrop, demanding of me sensitivity to the public reverberations of my behavior. And yet, the yardstick *of Kiddush Ha-shem* remains, in the end, a standard of measure fundamentally inward in nature.

This inwardness, however, is not tantamount to subjectivity. It remains resolutely intersubjective—and not just because of the presence of the communal glance. Its intersubjectivity is established at the deepest level by the presence of the Divine. And yet, this "solitude-of-two," as Rosenzweig so aptly coined the term, by its very nature appears to the person who beholds it from outside (which is everyone except me) as tenuous, if not illusory.[23] Rosenzweig warns that shyness must envelop this solitude-of-two: any attempt to communicate to a third party its immediacy and intimacy will merely highlight the chasm which cannot be breached: it was an experience that has already transpired, and it transpired in the intimate space between the Divine and me. For this reason, it is a solitude-of-two. So we might term the inwardness that the demand of *Kiddush Ha-shem* spawns objective, or rooted, inwardness. This is an inwardness of uncompromising demand, one that demands attentive hearing to the voice of the divine command, and a resolute willingness to heed its call—even if it leads to a break from the communal norm.

Rabbi Mordechai Lainer of Icbiza (the "Mei Shiloah") offers a powerful formulation of this experience of the Divine in describing the rare, but spiritually- and halakhically-necessary moment at which I ask myself whether I must violate the halakhic norm in order to fulfill the divine will, the deeper divine command that remains buried, and therefore hidden, beneath the mountain of halakhot. In order to make such a determination that the calling that I am experiencing is genuinely divine in origin, I must proceed along a rigorous path of examination in which I test my will and my understanding time after time, and if I arrive at the tenth station, totally purged of any self-serving desire, I can and must understand the demand to be divine in origin—despite the discrepancy between it and the communal norm.[24]

But the wider reverberations of this private determination cannot be blurred: precisely because *Kiddush Ha-shem* is meaningful only in a public or communal context, the possibility of needing to violate the established norm is of such consequence.

*Kiddush Ha-shem* is thus fraught with risks. At the most basic level, the risk inheres that I may mishear the command of the Divine. Furthermore, my act of *Kiddush Ha-shem*, in the case that it stands in opposition to the communal norm (at least in the short term), risks appearing to be just its opposite, *Ḥillul Ha-shem*, desecration of the divine name. Paradoxical as it may sound, *Ḥillul Ha-shem* may transform into *Kiddush Ha-shem* as the authenticity of the experience of the Divine is verified or as communal perspective on the deed undergoes change. This possibility that *Kiddush Ha-shem* may, in the short term, appear to be *Ḥilul Ha-shem*, in turn, yields another risk: namely, that even if I have heard the command accurately, I may not have the courage to comply, knowing that doing so will entail social conflict and alienation from the community.

## From Mythic Community to Communities in Maḥloket

Truth be told, this social conflict and alienation are not risks exclusive to *Kiddush Ha-shem*. Social conflict and, more precisely, confrontation, are the inherent risks and necessary costs of the halakha per se.[25] Acting upon the divine command, living out a command, transforming the spoken word into deed necessarily involve confrontation. Just as choosing the words involves saying "no" to many possibilities of thought that are—until that moment—indeterminate, transforming the word into deed involves a breaking point, the crossing of a threshold, a thrusting of oneself into the direction of one interpretation, one manifestation, one actualization of that word.

This rupture is called maḥloket, and it is one of the stalwarts of the halakhic system. We stake ourselves, our lived existence, on a particular understanding of the divine command, and with this determination we declare our belonging—not to the mythic halakhic community, but to a particular halakhic community. The deepest intuition of the rabbis was that the halakha—precisely for its wholeness—needs a multiplicity of lived interpretations.[26]

For this reason, the Mishna in Hagiga (2:2) lists a disagreement that continues for four generations of sages ("the pairs," as they are known), until the generation of Hillel and Menahem. For four generations, one authoritative sage holds that one must not place one's hands on the *hagiga* sacrifice while a different authoritative sage holds that one must, in fact, do so. Hillel and Menahem, the Mishna tells us, agreed on this point of halakha. So important is the mere fact of their agreement that the Mishna does not even bother to tell us what position both agreed upon. Suddenly, and without explanation, Menahem departs and Shammai takes his place, doing what he knows to do best: disagreeing with Hillel. Once disagreement has been established, the conversation can continue.

The only thing that is solitary—truly one—is the Divine. Even the Divine's names are many, which is why we look to the truly redemptive moment as the one when the Divine is one *and* the Divine's name is one. Various rabbinic traditions would have it that the divine word—mythically understood—was also one: the Divine only uttered the word אנכי [*anokhi*], I.[27] But even according to this understanding—and certainly according to the more "conventional" understandings—as speech emerges from the shrouds of the divine unity, seeking a temporary repose in the open field of human language, the words become many. And though the words congeal to form a whole, a unity of their own, the Torah becomes two: the written Torah and the oral Torah. For the rabbis it is at once unavoidable, a cause of celebration, and a source of angst that the interpreted word of Torah fractures into 70 splinters, spinning into multiplicity.

So it should come as no surprise that the lived-out word, word-as-deed—that is, the halakha—achieves neither unity nor unanimity. "The halakhic community" is a composite of halakhic communities—an interrelated conglomerate of communities that argue through deed. The communities amalgamate into a unity—they are "one" community—in the sometimes friendly, always impassioned bickering of their diversely-lived lives, as each of them plays out its understandings of a life of service to the Divine. Israel, too, forms a composite one—a variegated oneness of which "the halakhic community" forms a part.

Those of us in need of certainty in our lives—especially in our spiritual lives—cannot easily accept this rabbinic vision of what it means to live out a spiritual life with a thorough committedness, the kind that usually characterizes only those whose religious devotion is grounded in a myth (or illusion) of certainty. But the rabbis are uncompromising—one might even say zealous—in their commitment to distinguish between an authentic and devoted religious practice, on the one hand, and epistemological certainty, on the other. In an intricate, hard-hitting, sprawling discussion, they insist, time and again: but surely Beit Shammai did not actually live out their understanding of the halakha![28] For once the halakha was determined as going according to Beit Hillel—twice, really (once because Beit Hillel outnumbered Beit Shammai, and once because a divine voice issued from the heavens uttering that the halakha is according to Beit Hillel)—surely after that Beit Shammai conceded for the sake of the unity of the halakhic community. After all, asks the Talmud, how can we be one community if some people celebrate Purim on one day while others celebrate it on another? Or, more pointedly and more painfully, how can we constitute one community if we disagree (as Beit Hillel and Beit Shammai did in the most thorough of manners) regarding issues of personal status: what comprises legitimate marriage, what comprises divorce, what are legitimate offspring, and so on? The Talmud faces head-on the very same questions of identity and communal borders that spark acerbic arguments to this day: is this person a legitimate Jew? Can I marry her? Can I eat her food? Faced with disagreements of such dire consequence, the Talmud reasons, Beit Shammai surely must have understood the destructive potential inherent in fracturing the community. The Talmud reasons that Beit Shammai no doubt accepted their obligation to preserve unity, deferring to Beit Hillel's determinations! But the flow of the Talmudic discussion belies such assumptions. For three-and-a-half pages (seven folios), line after line, proof after proof, example after example, the Talmud tries to achieve the victory of unity—which is to say, religiously and epistemologically speaking, the tranquility of certainty—but the failure is as complete as it is protracted. As Rabbi Yoḥanan insists at the beginning of the discussion, Beit Shammai עשו ועשו [asu ve'asu]—they most certainly did act according to their own understanding of the halakha! Or, as the last five lines of the passage insist in a way that leaves the reader as certain as she is exhausted, "Hear clearly: [Beit Shammai] did [act according to their understanding of the halakha]; hear clearly!"

The rabbis are steadfast in their insistence upon the religious authenticity of the individual: if I understand the divine command to demand action, my very being is at stake. Nay, even more: the Divine is at stake. At these extreme moments, I must risk violation of the accepted norm and the excoriation that necessarily ensues. "It is the time to act for the Divine, for they have violated your Torah," writes the Psalmist.[29] But Rabbi Natan puts a spin on the verse, reversing its sequence and with it the ensuing logic: "They needed to violate your Torah because it was time to act for God."[30] Violation of the accepted norm, the Torah, sometimes reflects a deeper allegiance to the Divine: a fulfillment of the divine will, rather than a rejection of it. Or in the words of Rabbi Shimon ben Lakish: At times, the nullification of the Torah is its very foundation.[31]

Would I, could I, compromise what the Divine asks of me for the sake of some mythic communal unity? Surely not. I will—as Beit Shammai and Beit Hillel did, according to the Talmudic accounting cited—figure out creative ways to live alongside members of the extended halakhic community with whom I disagree. That commitment to not letting our communities drift apart entirely is the deepest meaning of the unity of "the halakhic community." It is a constant calling and a reminder that we must, as communities and as individuals, remain in steadfast awareness—an awareness that will necessarily breed humility—that we are all, despite the diversity of our understandings and actions, orienting the entirety of our being around an attempt to live the life of holiness that the Divine—in its infinite and inaccessible unity—commands.

## EXITING THE CONFINED COMMUNITY

Maḥloket ensures that at the core of the halakhic life there exists a gnawing awareness that my community's lived halakha has yet to become the exclusive practice of the halakhic community broadly conceived.[32] Moreover, the halakha has yet to become the framework for all Jewish action: large swaths of the Jewish community act in disregard or defiance of the halakha. And beyond the narrow confines of the Jewish people, the halakha has the most minimal of aspirations. This progression outward through concentric circles occurs simultaneously with a resolute, unabated commitment to my understanding of what the halakha commands of me. At once, two moves transpire: one casts a glance outward, while the other, an uncompromising inwardness. This synchronicity points toward one of the great tensions of Jewish life: its incessant, pulsating movement—at times jerky, to be sure— between two moments, the particular and the universal. Within the confines of the halakha, the ineluctable draw of each pole is undeniable.

First and foremost, the halakha is here and now. The halakhic authority is called the מרא דאתרא [*mara d'atra*]—the master of the place. Local custom has the status of halakha.[33] The laws of Shabbat weave a fabric of time and place that creates a locality in which my spiritual world is grounded. The laws of צדקה [*tzedaka*] draw these concentric circles in the world of ethical obligation: I am first obligated to give tzedaka to the one in need who is close to me, then to the one in my town, then to the one who is a part of my people, then to the one who is not.[34]

But justice knows no boundaries, and the image of the Divine is not limited to subgroups of humanity: why would I care for a Jew who lives next door to me more than a Jew who lives in the next town? Why would I care more for someone Jewish more than someone who is not? Levinas—with his attention to the face of the other—realizes that a world in which I throw myself prostrate before the infinite demand of another is a world in which the injustice of myopia prevails. My neighbor's demand is infinite, but so is the demand of the next-in-line, and the one after, as well. And so we must enter into the fray of political considerations and moral discourse.[35] This-worldly existence—and what is the halakha after if not bringing holiness into this-worldly existence?—requires an honest awareness that my locale is merely local, but that it is part of a wider nexus of existence.

The rabbis, too, were keenly aware of this conundrum. Hillel famously posed: If I am not for myself, who will be for me? But if I am only for myself, what am I? Precisely this same tension exists at the level of the collective. And so מפני דרכי שלום [*Mipenei Darkei Shalom*]—because of the ways of peace—we allow heathens to gather gleanings from our field, we give alms to both heathen and Jewish indigents, we pay visits to sick heathens just like we do for ill Jews, and we bury their dead alongside ours.

The cynical reading would suggest that the rabbis cared exclusively about Jews but were afraid to play out their ethnocentrism fully "because of the ways of peace"—that is, so that they could have decent relations with non-Jews. But a closer look indicates that it is (even) the weak non-Jews for whom we must care; it is the indigent and powerless non-Jews whom we must feed; the feeble and sickly non-Jews whom we visit; the deceased non-Jews to whose burial rites we attend. Thus the rabbinic turn of phrase "ways of peace" demands that we leave the confines of our community. We relinquish the natural and healthy allegiances of particularity and recognize that deeper ties of humanity transcend communal borders. Within the halakha is a passageway through which we exit the narrow confines of the system, internalizing the ideal of peace that exists alongside the inclination and need to create the localized bonds of community.

Put otherwise, the consideration of "ways of peace" leads into an open expanse within the halakhic system in which we are commanded to attend to those who are external to the system. Indeed, we encounter in this fertile region of the halakha a recurrent demand to internalize the glance of those who are external to the system. The halakha tries to adopt within its confines an Archimedean point from which, as it were, we can stand on the outside and glance at the halakhic norm—and at those who abide by it. "And you shall keep and observe [the divine statutes and laws] because they are your wisdom and your understanding in the eyes of the nations, who will hear of these laws and say, 'How wise and understanding is this great nation'" (Deuteronomy 4:6). The Torah expects its laws to be intelligible—and therefore meaningful—to those who are not subject to its commands. In fact, the laws are to be a source of admiration and inspiration for those who gaze upon it! Quoting this verse, Maimonides, jurist and philosopher, drives this point home in his *The Guide of the Perplexed*.[36] As he points out, many people are driven by exactly the opposite religious intuition: namely, they hold that the more esoteric the law and the less sense it makes to someone outside the system, the greater is its religious authenticity, the more convincing the proof of its divine nature. Maimonides, by contrast, poses precisely the opposite standard of religious authenticity: the halakha demands that it be intelligible—even inspirational—to those outside the system.

Knowing this, observers of the halakha walk the earth with an internalized third eye—one that seeks to glance upon their own actions from without, questioning whether the life that they are living arouses admiration among those who do not adhere to it. *Kiddush Ha-shem* becomes a vector which extends from a person's innermost point—my aloneness-together in moments of intimacy with the divine—and from there extends outward to my surrounding Jewish community, still further out to the Jewish community at large, and even further still to those outside of the Jewish community. In this way, the power unleashed by the category of *Mar'it Ayin*—the penetrating glance of the person who observes my actions—plays out well beyond the confines of the Jewish community.

Halakhic piety demands a concomitant attention to these two centrifugal forces whose pulls can never be resolved, only managed: the local and the global. It knows of no possibility of arriving at commitment to humanity without commencing with a commitment to my environs: the people of Israel. Michael Walzer's description of the nature of moral interpretation offers an apt portrait of the halakhic trajectory. Arguing in contradistinction to the possibility of moral "discovery" posited by Thomas Nagel, Walzer suggests that we do indeed have the possibility of "stepping back" from our local situation, but we cannot step back all the way to "nowhere."[37] Being committed halakhically entails a willingness-obligation to pursue an ever-receding horizon of commitment, while affirming the ability-obligation to keep one's feet rooted firmly here, now.

My desire to live a life of truth may be uncompromising; my commitment to humanity, borderless; my longing to cleave to the Divine, infinite. But the discrete act is not desire, neither is it commitment or longing; it is individuated action. And so the halakha, in its impulse to give the infinite expression and presence in the here-and-now, takes the individual, ever-attendant to the nuanced command of the divine voice, and thrusts her into the nexus of communal praxis. It then juxtaposes the lived halakha of that particular community with the differing determinations of other halakhic communities. Finally, it demands of the halakhic community, broadly conceived—which is to say, of each individual in each halakhic community—to view itself from without. The unbridgeable chasm between what is most private—our ongoing conversation with the Divine through deed—and the unavoidably public nature of each and every deed which, qua deed, is subject to scrutiny—must not only be minded, it must be traversed. Because the Torah was given to human beings, and not to angels, the halakha, Torah-as-deed, will settle for nothing less.

## Notes

1. Robert Cover, "Nomos and Narrative" in *Harvard Law Review*, Volume 97 Number 8, 1983–1984; see also *Narrative, Violence, and the Law: The Essays of Robert Cover*, edited by Martha Minow, Michael Ryan, and Austin Sarat (Ann Arbor: University of Michigan, 1995). For excellent explorations of how the rabbis did this, see Moshe Simon-Shushan, *Stories of the Law: Narrative Discourse and the Construction of Authority in the Mishnah* (New York: Oxford, 2013); Barry Wimpfheimer, *Narrating the Law: A Poetics of Talmudic Legal Stories* (Philadelphia: University of Pennsylvania Press, 2011); and Rachel Adler, *Engendering Judaism: An Inclusive Theology and Ethics* (Boston: Beacon, 1999), 21 ff.
2. "A generation is growing up in an atmosphere of mere phrases and catchwords, and a kind of go-as-you-please Judaism is being created out of the breath of empty words. Our cries are nationalism, revival, literature, creation, Hebrew education, Hebrew thought, Hebrew labor. ... But where is duty? Whence can it come? On what is it to live? On *Aggadah*? ... What we need is to have duties imposed on us! ... We long for something concrete. Let us

learn to demand more action than speech in the business of life, *Halacha* than *Aggadah* in the field of literature." Ḥaim Naḥman Bialik, *Halacha and Aggadah* from *Revealment and Concealment: Five Essays*, trans. Leon Simon, (Jerusalem: Ibis Editions, 2000), 86.

3. See Steven M. Cohen, Ron. Miller, Ira M. Sheskin, Berna Torr, "Campworks: The Long-Term Impact of Jewish Overnight Camp," 2011, sponsored by the Foundation for Jewish Camp (FJC). It can be accessed online at http://www.jewishdatabank.org/Studies/details.cfm?Stud yID=566

4. *Franz Rosenzweig: His Life and Thought*, ed. Nahum N. Glatzer (Philadelphia: JPS, 1953), 246.

5. Mishnah Rosh Hashana 2:9.

6. See Chap. 1, note 14.

7. "The seventh day is a *palace in time* which we build. It is made of soul, of joy, and reticence. In its atmosphere, a discipline is a reminder of adjacency to eternity." Abraham Joshua Heschel, *The Sabbath: Its Meaning for Modern Man* (New York: Farrar, Straus and Giroux, 1988), 14–15. Emphasis in original.

8. "There are two [types of] transfers on Shabbat which amount to four inside, and two which amount to four outside. How so? The indigent person stands outside and the homeowner is inside: [If] the indigent person reaches his hand inside and puts something into the hand of the homeowner, or takes something from [the hand] and brings it outside, the indigent person is liable and the homeowner is exempt. [If] the homeowner reaches his hand outside and puts [something] into the hand of the poor person, or takes [something] from [the hand] and brings it inside, the homeowner is liable and the indigent person is exempt. [If] the indigent person reached his hand inside and the homeowner takes [something] from it, or puts [something] into it, and [the indigent person] brings it outside, they are both exempt. [If] the homeowner reaches his hand outside and the indigent person takes [something] from it, or puts [something] into it, and [the homeowner] brings it inside, they are both exempt" (Mishna Shabbat 1:1).

9. For a longer exploration of these ideas, see my "Shabbat as Holiness in Spacetime" in *Kikar Ha-Ir*, Volume 2 (Tel Aviv, forthcoming) [Hebrew].

10. B.T. Eruvin 13b.

11. B.T. Bava Batra 60b.

12. B.T. Shabbat 88b.

13. B.T. Kiddushin 54a.

14. Nathan Englander, *For the Relief of Unbearable Urges*, (New York: Knopf, 1999).

15. B.T. Kiddushin 40a.

16. Martin Buber writes: "The men in the Bible are sinners, like ourselves, but there is one sin they do not commit – our arch-sin: They do not dare confine God to a circumscribed space or division of life." *The Martin Buber Reader: Essential Writings*, ed. Asher Biemann, (New York: Palgrave Macmillan, 2002), 162.

17. In his 1894 essay "Priest and Prophet," Ahad Ha-ʿAm writes: "There are two ways of doing service in the cause of an idea; and the difference between them is that which in ancient days distinguished the Priest from the Prophet." The Prophet "[i]s essentially a one-sided man. A certain moral idea fills his whole being. . . . He can only see the world through the mirror of his idea; he desires nothing, strives for nothing, except to make every phase of the life around him an embodiment of that idea in its perfect form." By contrast, the Priest "[a]ppears on the scene at a time when Prophecy has already succeeded in hewing out a path for its Idea. . . . The Priest also fosters the Idea, and desires to perpetuate it; but he is not of the race of giants. He has not the strength to fight continually against necessity and actuality. . . . Instead of clinging to the narrowness of the Prophet, and demanding of reality what it cannot give, he broadens his outlook, and takes a wider view of the relation between his Idea and the facts of life. Not what *ought* to be, but what *can* be is what he seeks." Ha-ʿAm, *Selected Essays of Ahad Ha-ʿAm*, 130–131.

18. B.T. Yoma 86a.

19. Franz Rosenzweig, *Der Mensch und Sein Werk: Gessamelte Schriften, B.1.2, Briefe und Tagebücher*, Dordrecht: Martinus Nijhoff, 1984, 789 [German].

20. B.T. Sanhedrin 74b.

21. Immanuel Kant, *Groundwork of the Metaphysic of Morals*, trans. H.J. Patton (New York: Harper, 1964), 103–107.

22. B.T. Shabbat 64b, Avodah Zarah 12a.

23. Rosenzweig in *Franz Rosenzweig: His Life and Thought*, 243. Glatzer translates the phrase "aloneness-together," but I prefer my own "solitude-of-two," both in terms of its fidelity to the German and in terms of the reality it manages to convey.

24. Rabbi Mordechai Lainer of Icbiza, *Mei HaShiloakh*, Part I, Parashat Pinkhas, 44a [Hebrew]. Ariel Evan Mayse has written a number of excellent articles that explore the contours of Hasidic halakha in which these issues are salient. See Maoz Kahana and Ariel Evan Mayse, "Hasidic *Halakhah*: Reappraising the Interface of Spirit and Law," *AJS Review* 41.2 (forthcoming, 2017); Ariel Evan Mayse, "Neo-Hasidism and the Theology of *Halakhah*: The Duties of Intimacy and the Law of the Heart" in *A New Hasidism: Branches*, ed. Arthur Green and Ariel Evan Mayse (Jewish Publication Society/University of Nebraska Press, forthcoming 2018), and Ariel Evan Mayse, "The Ever-Changing Path: Visions of Legal Diversity in Hasidic Literature" in

*Conversations: The Journal of the Institute for Jewish Ideas and Ideals* 23 (2015), 84–115.

25. Joseph B. Soloveitchik, "Confrontation," in *Tradition: A Journal of Orthodox Thought* 6 (1962). See also B.T. Berakhot 10b-11a.

26. For an excellent secondary source on the matter, see Avi Sagi, *The Open Canon: On the Meaning of Halakhic Discourse*, trans. Batya Stein (NY: Continuum, 2007), especially Parts 2, 3, and 4.

27. Numerous rabbinic sources, including B.T. Makot 23b-24a, B.T. Horayot 8a, and *Song of Songs Rabba* 1:2, suggest that at Sinai the Divine only issued forth the first two commandments, those that in fact contain no command but are merely the Divine's identifying of the Divine self. Later traditions would have it that the Divine only uttered the first word of the commandments "I," and Rabbi Menakhem Mendel of Rimanov allegedly teaches that the Divine only uttered the letter א [*alef*] of אנוכי [*anokhi*]. See Zeev Harvey, "Mah BeEmet Amar HaRebbi MiRimanov al HaAlef shel 'Anokhi' in *Kabbalah: Journal for the Study of Jewish Mystical Texts*," ed. Daniel Abrams, Volume 34 (Los Angeles: Cherub, 2016), 297–314 [Hebrew].

28. B.T. Yevamot 13b-17a.

29. Psalms 119:126.

30. Mishnah Berakhot 9:5, B.T. Berakhot 63a.

31. B.T. Menaḥot 49a-49b.

32. Nearly all treatments of Franz Rosenzweig's approach to halakha mention his use of the term "not yet" in the context of donning *tefillin* and fasting (Rosenzweig, Letter to Rudolf Hallo on March 27, 1922), in *Der Mensch und Sein Werk: Gessamelte Schriften, B.1.2*, 765 [German]. However, as I argue in my book *U've'Lekhtekha VaDerekh*, Rosenzweig's use of the term "not yet" carries with it deeper philosophical and theological implications. See Rosenzweig, *Star of Redemption*, 184–185 and my *U've'Lekhtekha VaDerekh: Teoria shel HaHalakha Al Basis Mishnato Shel Franz Rosenzweig* (Ramat Gan: Bar Ilan University Press, 2017) [Hebrew], 83–84, 151–156.

33. For a good overview, see Menachem Elon, *Jewish Law: History, Sources, Principles*, trans. Bernard Auerbach and Melvin J. Sykes (Philadelphia: The Jewish Publication Society, 1994), Chapters 21 and 22. See also Chapter 12.

34. "Rav Yosef taught ...: If your poor person, meaning one of your relatives, and one of the poor of your city come to borrow money, your poor person takes precedence. If it is between one of the poor of your city and one of the poor of another city, the one of the poor of your city takes precedence" (B.T. Bava Meẓia 71a). See also Maimonides, *Mishneh Torah*, The Laws of Gifts to the Poor, Chapter 7 Halakha 7 through Chapter 9 for his discussion of how to prioritize the allocation of tzedaka.

35. Emmanuel Levinas, *Totality and Infinity: An Essay on Exteriority*, trans. Alphonso Lingis, (Pittsburgh: Duquesne University Press, 1969), 212–215.

36. Moses Maimonides, *The Guide of the Perplexed*, trans. by Shlomo Pines (Chicago: University of Chicago, 1974), Volume Two, 523ff. (Corresponds to Part III, Chapter 31).

37. Thomas Nagel suggests that "since we are who we are, we can't get outside of ourselves completely. Whatever we do, we remain subparts of the world with limited access to the real nature of the rest of it and of ourselves. There is no way of telling how much of reality lies beyond the reach of present or future objectivity or any other conceivable form of human understanding" [Thomas Nagel, *The View From Nowhere* (New York: Oxford University Press, 1986), 6]. Michael Walzer, expanding on both the possibilities and limits of attempts at objectivity, states: "I do not mean to deny the reality of the experience of stepping back, though I doubt that we can ever step back all the way to nowhere. Even when we look at the world from *somewhere else*, however, we are still looking at the world. We are looking, in fact, at a particular world; we may see it with special clarity, but we will not discover anything that isn't already there" [Michael Walzer, *Interpretation and Social Criticism* (Cambridge: Harvard University Press, 1987), 7].

# CHAPTER 4

# The Ineffable

**Abstract** This chapter provides a phenomenological theology of command. Within the complex and diverse ecosystem of the halakha, the beating heart that sends the pulse of life to its farthest parts is the Divine. Working with two concepts central to the rabbinic concept of devotion, *yir'ah* (awe) and love, Wiener Dow illuminates how each offers a path to—and from—the command. While *yir'ah* seems eminently compatible with a commanding voice, love, too, finds its rightful place in the experience of commandedness, offering the "underbelly of the life of command." The halakha's uncompromising insistence that the individual drag the private experience of the Divine into the daylight of intersubjective (and intercommunal) reality reveals it to be a praxis that points at possibilities of authentic religious existence beyond its borders.

**Keywords** Negative theology • God and the halakha •
The Tetragrammaton • *ahava* and *yir'a*, love and awe/fear •
halakha and Jewish existence

Because Torah was given to human beings, mortals, its destiny—its future—is inextricably linked to time. The Divine gave itself over to Israel along with the Torah—so the Torah teaches.[1]

The Torah thus affirms what we already know from our everyday experience: time leaves its indelible imprint on each and every understanding we

© The Author(s) 2017
L. Wiener Dow, *The Going*,
https://doi.org/10.1007/978-3-319-68831-2_4

have. This includes our theological musings—even those understandings of the Divine as eternal, immutable, or exempt from the sways of time. So it is with my own musings: Yesterday He was God; today I speak of the Divine; tomorrow—? The edifice of theological understanding I build this morning will be cracked by mid-afternoon or evening.

If it were true to form, this would be a short chapter. What can I say about the ineffable? לך דומיה תהילה [*Lekha dumiyya tehilla*], said the master of the Psalms: To You, Silence is Adoration.[2] Every positive statement about the Divine furthers us from a proper understanding, Maimonides teaches.[3] But perhaps, instead of being appropriately short, this chapter will be intolerably long, as I try to capture in words, ever so briefly, that which immediately fades into an infinite horizon and, as I realize that I have not achieved contact, I approach from yet another angle. The halakha's great wisdom, I claimed in the previous chapter, is to give expression to that which issues forth from the ineffable: to put in action that which refuses to be bound in words. So why try to put into language that which eludes it?

There is a way in which language can chip away at that which lies beyond its grasp. On rare occasions, prose can do this. More often, midrash and poetry, with their indissoluble wedding of form and content, manage to do what prose cannot. As their form rubs irritatingly, provocatively, and stimulatingly against the grain of common syntax, they occasionally succeed in bursting out into the wide-open beyond language.

Poets and masters of midrash find a way to express the "aloneness-together" to which Rosenzweig alluded. Knowing that the experience of intimacy with the Divine sounds like an illusion to any third party, Rosenzweig conceded his position to that of the patient on the couch of the psychologist: why did you blab if you didn't want to submit yourself to analysis?[4] Similarly: why say something—anything—that will be incomplete; inferior to poetry; and a mere temporary formulation that will outgrow its own garb in which I dressed it and be in need of revision by the time the book goes to press—or perhaps, even for the reader, by the time she arrives at the end of the chapter?

The theological river may be impassable, but we must nonetheless enter its waters, for they flow as subterranean channels beneath the halakhic system. The halakha is a complex ecosystem: lived traditions, preserved counter-traditions; written laws, written dissents; lived norms alongside violations and adaptions of those norms; constant flux between custom and law; interwoven acts of legislation and interpretation; divergent communities of those observant; people unobservant who lie beyond the scope of the community but nonetheless stand in relation to it; rabbinic leadership, lay leadership, teachers, followers, protesters; ongoing learning and teaching that weave themselves into a fabric of ever-expanding Torah, which in turn demands expression; seekers from within the community who venture to its border and beyond, returning to the fold with new wisdom, alongside seekers from outside who join the community in an effort to express holiness in deed.

At every level of the system; nestled deep into all of its fissures and erupting onto its open spaces; above it all, underneath it all, and enveloping it in its entirety; casting light from without and glowing from within: issues forth the silent voice and the constant presence of the nameless one, offering a command that is both point of departure and telos, providing orientation as well as direction, grounding as well as trajectory. To root the action in the here and now, to fulfill the commandment today, in the present moment, requires an awareness and an acknowledgment of this presence. This chapter is my effort to testify to the presence of this presence.

How can I testify to this presence without naming it? The shortcut is tempting: God. My teacher, Rabbi David Hartman, would tell of an incident when he was a congregational rabbi in Montreal. He was at the supermarket when he noticed one of his congregants who seemed to be avoiding him. They met haphazardly as both turned the corner of an aisle with their carts. The congregant stammered and said: Rabbi Hartman, I really enjoy your sermons, but I haven't been to shul in a long time because . . . I don't believe in God. Rabbi Hartman smiled, paused, and told him: The God that you don't believe in I don't believe in, either.

Gabriel Marcel put a similar idea in philosophical garb, writing: when we speak of God, it is not of God that we speak.[5]

I prefer to speak of "the Divine" rather than of "God." An adjective is not an it, and never can be one, even if we seem to have transformed the adjective to a noun by attaching a definite article. But what I gain philosophically by this move, I lose theologically—for one cannot address an adjective. And part of standing in relation to the Divine is to be over against the Divine (מול [mul]—what Buber called Gegenüber in German), thrown into direct relation by a chasm that forms a connective separation between us. To turn my countenance toward the Divine requires an ability to address the one that can never be named. And yet—the Jewish tradition teaches that the Divine has many names. Elohim. Ha-Makom (the place!). El Shadai. The Creator. The Blessed Holy. The Master of the Universe. But one of the names marks the Divine as the wholly other, the one who can never be named, for it is a name—so the tradition teaches us—that cannot be uttered.

What is in a name, what is in uttering a name?

A name is a word that does what no mere word can do. It cracks open the façade of the objective world, plastered over smoothly by language, reaching in and pulling out its "object" into the bright light of the living.[6] In so doing, the name transforms the formerly-one-among-many into the subject of my address: No longer "thing," no longer "it," and not even a "you"—for the "you" cannot, ultimately, designate the truly singular; the named one is entirely unique.

We cannot address other than through the name. The name, the private name, is the ultimate word of address, the only one that singles out the one. When she is addressed by her private name, she is not one in the crowd, and she is no longer "merely" a you. With the utterance of the private name, the revelation of speech achieves completion. Every act of speech is self-revelation, as that which was inside receives body and is born into the world. But in the utterance of the private name, I bind my inner being to the one whom I address. In uttering her name, I place myself in relation to her as my subject.[7]

Of course, the utterance of a name does not always transpire qua address. Sometimes it involves the imposition of a label; that is exactly what is at stake in Adam's naming of the animals: assertion of sovereignty.[8] The act of naming—and even calling out by name—can be an exertion of power rather than the establishment of relation. Could it be thus in our relation to the Divine? Might the divine name serve as a source of power and imposition on our part—even an act of reduction—rather than the establishment of relation?

The halakha is notably silent on issues of theology. Rabbi Yehoshua famously declares that the divine voice has no say in the determination of the halakha, insisting that only the reasoned discourse of the sages carries weight. The rabbis are so adamant in their position that, as they tell the story, upon hearing this declaration, the Divine laughs, admitting defeat.[9] Yet even setting aside this aggadic story, the untrained eye notices the near-total absence of theological discourse from traditional halakhic literature: tens and hundreds of thousands of pages of Mishna, Talmud, the codes, and responsa reveal scarcely a mention of the Divine. It is nothing short of remarkable that an entire religious legal system—one meant to address nearly every aspect of its adherents' lives and one predicated on its divine origins—contains no definitive theological statement. God has nothing to say in halakhic discourse, and halakhic discourse returns the favor by maintaining silence on questions of theology.

Against the backdrop of our previous discussion, we might offer a generous interpretation of this silence as the halakha's opting for the act rather than for speech. But when speech-act is of theological moment, the halakha's prescription of action necessarily reveals a theological stance. Such is the case with regard to the norms of utterance of the divine name. According to the Mishna in Yoma, when the high priest would utter the Tetragrammaton on Yom Kippur, the holiest moment in time, in the temple, the holiest spot on earth, the people would fall on their faces, seeking shelter from an experience so intense that they could not withstand it in all of its unmitigated power, much the way we avert our eyes from our partner in conversation when the words spoken or the look cast upon us threaten to crush us under their weight.[10] The Tetragrammaton remains totally inaccessible, shrouded in a tradition of aura that leaves it as the one name of the one and only, protected by a shield of unpronounceability.

In an effort to make a legal claim for the awesome potential tucked away deep in the recesses of the divine name, the halakha erects high barriers around the act that unleashes those powers: the utterance of the name. Not just anyone can utter the name, says Rabbi Tarfon.[11] The halakha rigorously maintains the unpronounceability of the divine name: "AdoShem." "Yud-kay-vav-kay." "Shem Havaya." "Ha-shem Ha-mefurash." Or—most often—simply "HaShem." The Name. The name I can't say so I just say "The Name."

But why maintain as unutterable the name of the very root of being, the ubiquitous and the timeless, who is with us, around us, against us, supporting us, at every moment, online and accessible, there-for-us and here-with-us 24/7/365? Why wouldn't absolute and unremitting presence translate into constancy in availability? Perhaps the halakha's act of refrain from uttering the divine name reflects a religious temerity, an unwillingness to invoke the Divine and unleash its awesome force? Or perhaps it reflects a false piety: I create for myself an aura of holiness and humility by refraining from what I could utter but forego out of deference to the communal norm.

But it is not about false piety. The structure that the halakha erects in the regulation of the divine name is not principally a towering wall designed to prevent the actual utterance of that four-letter word. It is rather a dam, constructed with masterful engineering prowess, in the great river of language that flows from the very source of being. Fending off the powerful force of the waters crashing against the most resolute—and oft-cited—of all names, the restrictions demand that each utterance of the divine name be sincere, a genuine appeal and address. The regulations seek to ensure that—at least with one word—I mean what I say. In so doing, they ensure the existence of any and every private name, a move which in turn vouchsafes the continued possibility of direct address between two subjects. And what flows between two subjects who address each other is speech, so it is speech itself whose possibility is guaranteed by the sparse word of the Name. By regulating the flow of the river Language, the dam thus allows its waters to continue to flow, irrigating the interminable chain of being.

The halakha requires fastidiousness in the utterance of the divine name precisely because doing so can never be an exertion of power; it can only be an invocation, for vis-à-vis the Divine I have no power to assert through the act of labeling. Precisely because of the constancy and the ubiquity of the Divine, the act of uttering the divine name is an appeal, a request, to transform the nature of the divine presence. I want to be able to address the Divine, an act that requires distance between us. It is an effort to enable the presence of the Divine to shift from archetypal mother to archetypal father. The "Mother" is the one who is with us all the time, a presence so constant that it is, at best, a blurred image at the edge of my consciousness, the sensing of a presence that is with me but not me. In the very act of acknowledging the presence of a presence, I allow the "Mother" who was with me all day to don the garb of the "Father" who arrives home and enters. I try to amalgamate the scattered light of the divine presence and concentrate it by refracting it through the lens of the word so that it forms a single beam—one that is visible to the naked eye. In this way, it assumes a temporary but rightful place across from me, over and against me. Distant from me. Other than me. With this separation comes the possibility of address, as the constant, inarticulate and ineffable constancy-presence has been transformed into a—a what? Could it ever be an it? A subject? A you? I can only say: it can be addressed, and the possibility of that address, the grounding of that address, the guarantee of that address, is encapsulated in the divine name.

But at this very moment of writing I am not attempting to address the divine. I am trying to articulate the sense of the divine that pulsates throughout the halakha, and it begins with the possibility of the direct address—and the "intersubjectivity" (for lack of a better term) that ensues, allowing for address, for calling, for listening, for commanding. But the halakha qua deed wants to say more than merely the divine name. It aspires to transform that constant, inarticulate presence into address-through-deed.

The life oriented around the halakha is a conscious and constant choice to address the Divine through the series of deeds that amalgamate into my lived life. That is, beyond the explicit moments in which the divine is addressed by name, the halakha is engaged in a constant address of the divine. This address is not to the ineffable name—the way in which the divine traverses into the realm of language—but rather to the Infinite One as quest.

Once the scattered light has been refracted into a single beam, the light of that beam strikes the world in the fleeting moment of the discrete act, boring a hole into the fabric of finite existence. And there, in and through that point, infinite light bursts into the finite world. Every deed can allow the light of infinity to seep in, however momentarily. No deed is expansive enough to contain the infinity of infinity.

The Talmud tells of someone who stepped forward to lead prayers in the presence of Rabbi Ḥanina. "The great, the mighty, the awesome, the majestic, the powerful, the awful, the strong, the courageous, the sure, the revered."[12] Rabbi Ḥanina waited until he finished and then asked him, "Have you finished enumerating the praises of your master [i.e., the Divine]?" Rabbi Ḥanina teaches that no words—however descriptive each one is, however many of them we string together—can suffice to exhaust the infinite. So, too, in the realm of halakha: no deed—or, for that matter, series of deeds—can open up a tear in the finite world wide enough to let in infinite light. For this reason, Herman Cohen and, following suit, Franz Rosenzweig, make use of the differential in their theologies. To invoke the divine is to approach infinity.[13] To approach necessarily means to be on a path of drawing near. A longing and a constant almost. Rabbi Naḥman of Breslav describes the experience of being distant from the divine as an indication of deep proximity.[14] This paradox can only hold if the experience of being distant results precisely from my proximity, from the constancy of the approach: I draw nearer, and as I draw nearer, the divine presence luring just over the unbridgeable chasm seems to draw nearer to my reach. But the unbridgeability of the chasm remains resolute.

Each finite deed reveals a glimpse of eternity, and an infinite number of finite deeds accomplish nothing more, offering nothing more than a glimpse. So the great word of the theology of the halakha is "and." This deed and that deed, strung together as a lived life, a life full of distinct moments that stand in varied relationships with one another: sometimes fulfilling, sometimes contradicting, sometimes overriding, sometimes receding, sometimes echoing, sometimes amplifying.

This deed and that deed also means: this deed of this person and the deed of that person; the deeds of this lived life and the deeds of that lived life; the deeds of this community and the deeds of that community. A chorus of voices, sometimes in pleasing harmony, sometimes in strident cacophony.[15] Yes, even the cacophony: just as the din of siblings fighting is an essential part of the noise of home, so too do disparate deeds form an essential whole through which the Divine is expressed, erecting walls that form separate rooms in the home in which the divine presence rests.

The "and" of the halakha points to the underlying oneness not only of the halakhic organism—the humanly erected structure aimed to serve as a dwelling place for the Divine; this great "and" also points to the oneness of the Divine.

Divine oneness as the halakha conceives and expresses it is not the oneness often found in Eastern "religions," where (what appear to be) distinct components of existence prove to unite in and be constituent parts of a deeper Oneness. The oneness expressed by halakha is the oneness of the havdallah candle. It is comprised of many wicks, but the flames join together—sometimes smoothly, sometimes in a jerky dance, sometimes joined by an intervening space—to form one flame. It is a oneness predicated upon separation, distinct wicks burning. And it dares to declare oneness at the conclusion of Shabbat—the gatekeeper of the secret of oneness.[16] What's more, it does so while staking out its ground at the very edge that divides—and in so doing also brings into contact—the oneness of Shabbat and the multiplicity of the six days of creation. Shabbat and the six days of creation. Oneness and division. Together, joined by the and, the oneness and the division form a greater oneness, one that, miraculously, includes the scattered pockmarks of division. The and of the halakha is the and of this greater oneness. To be committed to my way wholeheartedly, and to know that your ("wrong") way is part of the way, is to live out the "and" of the halakha, which in turn points to the great "and" of the Divine.

The oneness expressed by the halakha is the oneness of Jewish prayer. The staggering multiplicity of Jewish houses of worship is not merely occasion for self-mocking humor; it is an expression of what it means for the one people to testify to the one Divine and to approach it directly, head on. The one people splinters into multiple communities, each of which gathers to utter words of holiness that, according to halakhic regulative determination, can only be spoken in community, in the multiplicity of existence. Each community in its locale, each in its specific language, each at its own moment in the appointed hour—and to address the Divine.

But the staccato existence of houses of worship is merely a prelude to the teeming chaos that assaults the eye and ear of the person entering into any single one of these houses of worship. Neither meditative quiet nor speaking or singing in unison find more than a momentary dwelling here; a different cloth of connectivity forms the oneness. The leader reads the opening line of a section of the liturgy, but each member of the community proceeds to utter the words at her pace. Along the way, at the leader's behest, they may well join together in shared song, only to break apart once more. In the *Shema*, in which the Jew enjoins all of Israel to "Hear that the Divine, who is our God, is one," the eyes are closed as the visual community fades into an auricular one; the beginning of the declaration is uttered together, but then each community member proceeds at her pace. God's oneness is proclaimed by a great cacophony. In the moments leading up to the holiest of prayers, what the Talmud calls "the prayer," the community's voice gathers as they express the hope for redemption—and what can redemption be if not communal or worldly in nature?—only to transition to silence, yielding to the prayer of the individual, who whispers her words, loud enough to hear herself, quiet enough that her neighbor cannot. Each at her pace, each with her inflection, until—scouring the community, making sure that they leave no one behind—the leader assesses it is time to gather together in expression of *kedusha*: holiness. It is a moment of such gravitas that everyone within earshot must stand still: even a mere passerby, someone who is expressly not a part of that community of worship, must stop moving along her way, ceding to the power of the community that strives to express the unity of the holy, holy, holy.[17] The community expresses the holy by answering responsively—in part together, in part individually—the words of the leader. Together, the words of the individuals and the prayers of the community gather into one tapestry, a shawl of prayer that envelopes the community and expresses a larger oneness that is so great that it can contain, within itself, the absolute individuality, which is to say, the wholeness, the oneness—of each of its constituent components.

The "and" of the halakha also testifies to the oneness of the Divine as reflected in the lived lives of the Jewish people. The Jewish people amalgamate into one people—the one people, גוי אחד בארץ [*goy eḥad ba-aretz*].[18] The oneness of the Jewish people is neither a biological-ethnic-tribal fact, nor is it an aspirational desire, a kind of imagined communal oneness.

Neither is it a oneness determined by shared borders, shared language, or shared theology.

To the naked eye, it seems that the only sense of oneness that the Jewish people can muster—the only truly connective tissue that defines it as an entity—is a clannish, hollow commitment to continue to exist. This pale sense of oneness would explain the Jews who have lived their entire lives with no traceable manifestation of their Jewish identity, only to discover their Jewish commitment when they understand that their children's lives contain no sense of Jewish identity or commitment whatsoever: marrying someone non-Jewish or choosing not to circumcise their son are nonissues for them—and thus cause of angst for the parent. The possibility—and, for many, the reality—of being the last link in a chain of Jewish commitment delivers a jarring alarm that stirs them from their Jewish slumber. But to what do they awaken? Having lived a life devoid of all substantive Jewish expression, why does this parent, acting in good faith, object to this partic-ular chain of Jewish existence drawing to a close? What might explain this resistance to death? The Jewish people, after all, is not a living organism that hangs on to life out of biological impulse or even out of fear of death. Some deeper force is at work—one scantly understood, and, to the extent that it is understood, resistant to articulation.

Jews are resistant to allowing the Jewish people to die because, in ways that most of us cannot fully articulate, and in places of our individual and our collective beings that are shielded from the bright light of inquiry, we sense that there is a purpose to Jewish existence. In theological terms, this purpose is to serve as witness to the Divine,[19] in large part by warning against the constant lure of idolatry[20]; in social justice terms, it is to engage in the betterment of the world[21]; in cultural terms, it is to offer some invaluable contribution to human flourishing; in humanistic terms, it is to champion the infinite worth of the human being *qua* human being.[22] In whatever terms we conceive it, what animates the Jewish insistence on survival is the sense that there is a telos to Jewish existence. Beyond the will to survive is an insistence on, and commitment to, not mere Jewish existence, but lived Jewish existence. Jews disagree about the nature and purpose of that lived Jewish existence—for, alas, Jews disagree; disagree-ment is, after all, an essential aspect of Jewish discourse (Torah) and an essential aspect of Jewish doing (halakha). Yet the underlying commitment is to realizing through our lived lives a deep-seated commitment.

In this way, the oneness of the Jewish people is radically different from the *e pluribus unum* of the United States. The oneness of the Jewish people is neither that of a melting pot nor that of a multicultural society whose guiding principle is that of liberty as the guarantor of a just and harmonious diversity that allows many to live either as one or under one roof. Nor is it a oneness of a post-ethnic society that lauds hybridity as the panacea for the ills of division. The Jewish many remain distinct, pulling in different directions. Yet the Jewish many is not content to remain many; a centrifugal force works to form it into the one Jewish people. An absence of tension will be a clear indication that we have lost our way; that things have ceased to matter; that we have compromised our insistence that our lived existence has some greater purpose.

This astoundingly-diverse lived Jewish existence is, broadly understood, the "and" of the halakha. It is a oneness in a commitment to doing—in its insistence upon deed, in its rooting its being in the deed, in orienting ourselves around deed. This deed need not conform to given halakhic practice, nor must it even try to be in relationship with the halakha. The "and" of the halakha casts its net wide enough to include those who orient themselves around it; those who reject it; and those who ignore it, knowingly or unknowingly. The midrash tells us that the Divine doesn't mind our abandonment, so long as we cling to the Torah.[23] This can only be the case because to live out our lives in conversation with Torah—whether the nature of that conversation be agreement, muted argument, even vociferous rejection—is to illuminate our deed as animated by telos. The unity of that telos—the and which establishes the oneness of the Jewish people—is rooted in, and reflective of, the oneness of the Divine.

The great "and" of the halakha also brings under its auspices both the realm of the secular and the realm of the profane in its attempt to find, express, and worship the Divine. For this reason, Rabbi Simḥa Bunam finds a path to the Divine even in so-called lesser people, even when they are dwelling and dealing in matters thoroughly mundane. At that moment, they hold a hint of wisdom as to how to worship the Divine. The person who realizes this, says Rabbi Simḥa, needs no rabbi: the one who shows him the path of holiness is the one right there, with whom he is interacting. Every person, every endeavor, every moment leads to the Divine.[24] Levinas overwhelms us with the burden of infinite responsibility to the other—any other, every other—who becomes an instantiation of the infinite. But as demanding as Levinas is, Buber broadens the scope of the ethic: alterity belongs not just to the face that I encounter, but also to the tree in which I stand in relation. Lurking in Buber's description is—despite his best intentions—a normative discourse. The trees, the inanimate world, the animal kingdom—indeed, all of creation!—demand that I recognize them and treat them as products of creation and, as such, as carrying the imprint of the Divine.

So viewed, the finite world leads to incessant opportunities—and challenges—to reveal the Divine, infinite invitations to testify to the divine presence, innumerable obligations to offer the divine presence an avenue of expression. Each and every of our actions, as an interaction with the world but also as a contribution to the ongoing amassing of human endeavor, offers a way to refract the divine light. That is the halakhic task.

The "and" of the halakha is also the infinity of the halakhic life: a commitment that knows no end because—as testament to the infinite—it can have no end. Leibowitz often compared the halakhic life to that of a homemaker: to clean house is to know that there is no once-and-for-all: we put the toys away; return the books to the shelf; wash the dishes—only to have entropy-in-the-form-of-the-lived-life wreak its havoc the next day.[25] This "halakhic sobriety,"[26] as Hartman termed it, means that after the ecstasy of the closing Neilah service of Yom Kippur, after its pinnacle, in which we declare the Nameless One as the one and only: after all of this, the halakha makes an abrupt landing into the muck of reality. In a kind of postscript to the ecstatic expression of the presence of the One, an odd transition—perhaps regression is the better word—transpires: "Next year in rebuilt Jerusalem." On the surface, we are still in the redemptive mode of expression, offering an aspiration that may well reflect a sense that we have arrived. But the "next year" is an unavoidable slap across our face: only next year. Not yet. And so we immediately transition to the weekday evening service, including a request for divine forgiveness for the sins we have committed. Sufficient time has not elapsed for us to even manage another sin! We confess because to be a human living in the presence of the Divine is to be on the way. On the way to oneness, in a world of multiplicity.

But our muscles cannot be flexed indefinitely, and our eyes cannot see clearly in the blur of the rapid pace of movement, so the halakha demands a rest from being on the way. The rest commanded on Shabbat is not a "privilege" (though it feels like one), nor is it a functional rest designed to enable further labor during the six days of gathering the divine light (though it does, indeed, have that effect). It is the infinite of the depth of stasis within the infinite movement of the way.

The basic command of Shabbat is to relate to the world as illuminated: not as worthy of redemption, and not as capable of being redeemed in the future, but rather as containing "already-redeemed" in its depth. On this day, the task of the halakha is similar to the task of the "everyday" halakha, but without the movement toward the future. Everything, every one, every encounter offers not a way to refract the divine light, but rather an instantiation of the divine light. The halakha achieves this not by demanding a change of consciousness, but rather by effectuating a praxis of relation. A mosquito bites us, and we shoo it away rather than kill it; we do not trap animals, nor do we pull branches from trees or pick flowers. We cultivate relationship rather than exercise control: that is the overarching command of Shabbat. Levinas claims that "[v]iolence is to be found in any action in which one acts as if one were alone to act: as if the rest of the universe were there only to receive the action."[27] One day a week, the halakha fashions a world entirely absent of violence in this radical Levinasian sense. To refrain from killing the mosquito is to take painstaking care to see the world as enchanted, to see it as perfect, as a masterpiece, as infused through and through with the Divine.

As I try now, after Shabbat, to describe the experience of seeing the world as it exists as full of perfection, it seems to be an at best an aspirational spiritual discipline, and at worst, a lie. But as the Zohar teaches, the great secret of Shabbat is the secret of oneness.[28] The world is revealed as an enchanted garden precisely insofar as I experience—and effectuate—the divine oneness to which it testifies. Every Jewish prayer service concludes by expressing an aspirational longing for "that day when the Divine will be one and the divine name one."[29] The halakha fashions a 25-hour vessel in which that day erupts from within the week.

Remarkably, what allows me to see the unity of the world outside of me, what allows me to be in relation to the world instead of exercising power over it, is the turn inward to what the Sefat Emet calls my innermost point. Shabbat slows down the movement of the world by drawing concentric, progressive circles that limit the space that we can inhabit. The 2000 *amah* beyond which I cannot travel lead to a furious scramble to root me to my private domain. My home becomes my palace: nothing can be removed from it, and even the hand of the indigent cannot penetrate it.[30] The universe shrinks around me, closing in on me, enveloping me until—yielding to the command to bring myself to a position of rest—I settle in one spot and allow myself to sink into my place of repose. Instead of glancing outward in order to provide myself some combination of nourishment and distraction from my own inner noise, I turn inward and enable the noise of the outside world to fade into a buzz that allows me to listen to sounds and voices inaudible under the normal din of daily working conditions.

The movement slows, the focus draws inward, and the rattle of the profane fades to a muffled whimper. And just as the loss of one sense sharpens the acuity of others; and just as one's body, having reached the point of resistance in a stretch, only to discover—after holding ground delicately—that it is now capable of a deeper stretch: so, too, does the slowing down of movement and the quieting of Shabbat enable, condition, and invite a more profound place of repose. This downward spiral reveals an infinity of inner stasis.

From within this position of stasis the senses are heightened: vision clearer, hearing sharper, taste more complex, touch more delicate, smells more pungent.[31] This heightened experience leads simultaneously in two directions to two incompatible-yet-coterminous experiences. One direction leads to a path of wonder, awareness, and unqualified acceptance. To be infused with the Divine is to have perfection within—not as potential but as actuality. The heightened awareness of Shabbat serves as a filter, a lens, that enables us to see—and magnify—that perfection in each and every creature, in each and every element of creation, around us.

And yet, there is, simultaneously, a great "not yet": an awareness that the divine perfection within each aspect of creation has not yet infused the entirety of creation, nor has it reached its capacity even within each distinct creature; an awareness that Shabbat is a 25-hour vessel in which time continues to run its course, each period within Shabbat containing its own quality—a beginning of the cessation of movement, a fullness and richness to the cessation that knows no other moment, and a waning of the unique consciousness of Shabbat, with the bittersweet taste of the unparalleled glimpse of divine light at precisely the moments of full awareness of its fleeting nature; an awareness that in order to see, smell, and hear this extent of the Divine infused in creation, I need to perform an act of partial withdrawal. And with the "not yet," nestled deep within it, is a supreme command that has not yet become command but takes the form of an ineluctable desire that knows no rest: to refuse to accept the "not yet." The "not yet" must become "now." It is a holy impatience, at once an inability and an unwillingness to accept Shabbat as withdrawal, as partial, as momentary, as bordered. The great secret of Shabbat, the secret of oneness, boasts a deep-down knowledge that is at once prescient knowledge and command: that the oneness of Shabbat is not, cannot be, merely oneness of Shabbat and one Shabbat. To be truly one, it cannot know borders.

But there is no avoiding it. Every Shabbat has an outward border: it may be a palace in time, but it is still in time. Motzei Shabbat (Saturday night) comes; Shabbat departs. The ceremony of havdallah—separation—offers within minutes a virtuoso performance of theme and variation: oneness contains division within it, precisely for the sake of its wholeness. We depart the world of onenesss and enter its inner world of division, otherwise known as the six days of Creation. The time has come to create.

There is, to be sure, a sweetness of Shabbat whose fragrance lingers in the air. But I can no more remain in the nourishing confines of Shabbat than I can stay at home once I've reached adulthood and am ready to realize my higher self—out there, in the world. The infinity of Shabbat's inner stasis leads, miraculously, to an emergence outward. From within the inner quiet a voice sounds—a voice that speaks from within but is not mine. It is a voice at once calm and commanding, one that speaks with unparalleled transparency, whispering that all that is out there—right out there, just beyond me—demands my full presence.

How can I understand this voice that issues forth from a beyond that lies within? The story is told in the Talmud that during those moments of the people of Israel's spiritual stupor, in which they were seeing voices, the Blessed Holy One held Mount Sinai over their heads with an offer they could not refuse.[32] Either accept the Torah or I will drop the mountain on your head and return the world to chaos. That's not command, says Rabbi Yaakov bar Aha; that's coercion, and coercion, he claims long before Locke, renders the religious act meaningless. Even the command must be chosen, freely accepted, embraced, assumed.

By recasting the voices floating visibly in the air at Sinai into a voice whose commandedness threatens, the rabbis bring to the fore the challenge of a religious life oriented around command: how can a voice from without spark an authentic doing? For if our doing were not authentically ours, why would the Divine command it? It could only be of significance to the Divine because we could have rejected it, but instead chose it. The Divine's choosing us becomes, must become, our choosing the Divine command.

The Divine held the mountain over the heads of Israel at Sinai—but they freely accepted it, קיימו וקיבלו, *kiyyemu ve-kibbelu*, at the time of Esther, says the Talmud. During the time of Esther!?—that one book in the Tanakh when God is not mentioned, when Jews assert themselves as Jews and, as human beings, assume full responsibility for their well-being? That is when the rabbis understand the Jews to have accepted the Divine command? From the Divine's overwhelming and overbearing presence at Sinai, the rabbis jump over Jewish history and books of the Torah until they arrive at that moment when the Divine is most hidden. There, and only there, can the Torah be fully accepted, can mitzva be freely assumed, can—dare I say it?—the Divine's voice be fully heard? Only when the external manifestation of the Divine voice falls silent can the inner contours of the Divine voice be heard. Only when the demand-command ceases to threaten from without can the yoke of responsibility and responsiveness issue forth from within.

This movement—from without to within—does not simply transpire. It is made possible—and evoked—by an inner movement on my part. Everything is in the hands of heaven, except for the יראה [yir'a], awe, that we have toward heaven, says Rabbi Ḥanina.[33] Despite our intuition that our innermost attitude toward the Divine is determined from without—a function of our upbringing, our innate disposition, our amalgamated experiences, and so forth, in fact it is that over which we exercise the most control. What is this inner attitude that then effectuates the possibility of hearing the Divine?

At one level, it is an outward adjustment, the movement of the pen before it touches down on the paper. Says Raba the son of Rav Huna: the person who has Torah learning but does not have an attitude of awe is like a guardian who has the keys to the inner chamber but didn't receive the key to the outer courtyard.[34] To "have" Torah without yir'a can only be an illusion: that person does not in fact have the ability to approach Torah, to unlock its meaning. The Torah that he holds is not, in fact, Torah. The same words have a different meaning when the approach to them is through the gate of yir'a. Raba's warning applies to Torah, instruction, in the broadest sense, and in this broad sense all of the world is instruction. Every interaction, every moment, is poised to offer instruction. But our ability to access that instruction depends upon our opening the outer gate and entering through the courtyard of yir'a. Humble, attentive, open to surprise, replete with reverence, ready to receive direction, awed at the beauty of the moment, awed by the responsibility that it contains, anxious to pursue the path it beckons.

At another level, yir'a is an inwardness that gently, confidently, and completely overcomes any and all outward adjustments. Immediately after the words of Raba the son of Rav Huna regarding the person who has Torah but lacks yir'a, Rabbi Yanai declares: what a waste to build a gate around a courtyard if you have no courtyard! Yir'a is an inner courtyard, an inner expanse, that no behavioral directives can fashion from without. Studying Torah and keeping the halakha are incapable of generating the inwardness that grants them their very meaning. The inner workings of the inner chamber must be fostered and crafted from materials other than Torah and mitzvot. It is an echo chamber that is sealed to the approach from without. But in it, a voice reverberates: a voice issues forth, its powerful sound reverberates, and together—voice and echo—they break out, refusing, as they do, to be contained as inwardness. And the person inwardly attentive is left listening, sifting through the voices, struggling to distinguish authentic voice from its mere—and thus deceptive—reverberation. It is with this inwardness—and only with it—that it is possible to approach the command.

"To approach the command"? No, I cannot approach a command. I can hear a command, I can respond to a command, but I can only approach—dare I say it?—a commander. To hear the command is to acknowledge being addressed and to "know" in a way far deeper than "knowing" that there is an addresser; to hear the command is to understand that I must move, that my work is not done, that creation is left wanting; to hear the command is to know that I must strain to decipher what is being demanded of me; to hear the command is to hear commands from multiple sources, at varying decibels, many contradictory, all in competition with one another, and to merge them or to bring one to the fore while the others fade, or to realize that one is the true command at this very moment, in this very place, and to understand, to truly know, that it, and only it, must be done, even if I wonder if—while doing it!—I may be mishearing; to hear the command is to know that the eternal, for the sake of its very eternity, needs to be compacted into the moment of now; to hear the command is to know that the demand of eternity will be fashioned over the course of time but only determined, once and for all, as the demand of eternity, in the unreached future; to hear the command is to know that my deed will live for eternity, and that eternity will hold up the deed in its light, asking all to gaze upon it and inquire as to whether it is worthy of being eternalized; to hear the command is to accept the full and terrifying responsibility of deed, and the possibility of misdeed; to hear the command is to know that in my deed I not only respond to the commander, I fashion the commander; to hear the command is to hear the commander, and to be in the commander's presence; to hear the command is to know that I am worthy of address, of being commanded.

To hear the command is to hear the commander, and to be in the commander's presence; to hear the command is to know that I am worthy of address, of being commanded. To hold simultaneously both of these aspects of hearing the command is no small task. To do so is to hold

together the rabbinic understanding of service to the Divine as a collabora-
tion of *yir'a* and *ahava*, love.

My rabbi and teacher would often cite the verse שויתי ה' לנגדי תמיד (Psalms
16:8)—"I am ever mindful of the presence of the Divine"—as an expression
of the highest of spiritual aspirations: to foster a constant "God-intoxica-
tion," as he used to term it, an unceasing awareness of, and thirst for, the
presence of the Divine.[35] When the Divine's presence is a commanding
one—and how could it not be?—the overwhelming sense of the Divine
transpires within the framework of *yir'a*. Obligation and awe are familiar
partners.

To sense the commander by hearing the command is to be in a room,
back to the opened door, and feel with certainty the presence of someone
who has entered silently. The presence of the One who not only avoids your
direct line of vision; it does not even reach the remotest edge of your
peripheral vision. It is a presence whose palpability is at once overwhelming
and utterly incapable of being grasped. And in a way that is both counterintuitive and eminently understandable, this presence is all the more commanding precisely because of its hidden, mysterious nature. To feel the
presence is to be on edge, eager to respond; weary of falling into a slumber,
and weary of misstep. On edge; eager; weary; responsive: so it is when, over
against me, juxtaposed with my presence, is the commanding presence of
the Divine.

And yet, just as I may dare to leverage the presence of the Divine into the
foreground, into my direct line of vision, into the distilled "You" of the
blessing that boldly places me in a position of address, so, too, I may dare to
invert the distribution of power, the hierarchy, that inheres in the moment
of command. With a "mere" change in consciousness—a change in consciousness that is no mere act, but rather a consummate act of self-love and
of theological brazenness—I may recast the command, reclaim my deepest
self, and reformulate my relationship with the Divine. I may lay claim to
being worthy of address.

To be worthy of address by the Master of All That Is, the One whose
voice ineluctably commands, the Infinite in every dimension and direction,
the Ungraspable, the Ineffable, the Divine? What could possibly make sense
of such a nonsensical proposition? The only thing more difficult than the
concept of my being addressed is to make the preposterous suggestion that I
may be worthy of the address. What would it mean for any human being to
be worthy of address? More pointedly, given that I know intimately the

breadth and depth of my failings, what could it possibly mean for *me* to be worthy of address?

An absurd question can only elicit an absurd answer, and so is the case here: I am only worthy of address because the Divine loves me. And what makes me worthy of the love of the Divine? The love of the Divine is what makes me worthy of the love of the Divine. Or, put otherwise, I am not worthy because of me, or because of something I have done; the love of the Divine is a gift, nothing more.

"The Divine loves me"? The notion of the Divine loving me leaves my religious and intellectual sensibilities profoundly unsettled. And yet, my discomfort aside, it is undeniably—and fortunately—true that the rabbis offer a way to negotiate the presence of the Divine that differs from *yir'a*, an alternative path of commitment and responsiveness: the path of love.

Here, too, the rabbis approach theological issues from the back door. The rabbis talk not about the Divine loving us, but instead about our loving the Divine. This may represent an epistemological stance, but it also reflects their uncompromising commitment to the Biblical text. Given the central and unequivocal Biblical injunction to love the Divine, they simply cannot avoid it. Instead of ignoring the question, they deflect it: to love the Divine, they assert, is to perform the mitzvot out of love.[36] Time after time, in text after text, the contrast between performance of mitzvot based on *yir'a* and performance based on love yields the same picture. Service of the Divine informed by *yir'a*, in which awe, reverence, and fear go hand-in-hand, seems conditional, predicated upon a consciousness of my smallness and my dependence upon the Divine, as well as my subjection to Divine judgment. By contrast, a responsiveness born of love and motivated by it has nothing to say about reward or punishment, for that calculus cannot enter one's religious sight of vision if one never glances remotely in that direction. Job loses everything, property and children, without blaspheming, and Rabbi Akiva experiences the moment of his martyrdom as a joyous occasion to realize the obligation to love the Divine—for only here, at these moments of total incomprehension, can unconditional acceptance transpire.[37] This ideal of performing the mitzvot with total and holy disregard for the consequences of observance feels quintessentially Jewish,[38] and the rabbis offer this posture a stamp of theological authenticity, declaring this to be love of the Divine.

But lest the rabbinic sleight of hand deceive us, they have enjoined us to love the Divine by acting out of love. Yet what could stir us to such love? The deep-down answer—one that forces me to plumb the depths of my soul and try to explain what could move me to live a life of service and devotion informed and motivated by love for the Divine—can only be that one reality that I would prefer to relegate to a vacuous idea embraced by late-night televangelists and my would-be convertors: that the Divine loves me.

So I must ask again: is that not an absurd proposition—that the Divine loves me? What could that possibly mean? The rabbis leave to us the work of deciphering, but they have already left us a hint in their discussion about how it is that we love the Divine: by accepting the Divine fully, unconditionally.

What does it mean to love somebody? It means, first and foremost, to concede to the mystery of love. The very fact of love obliterates any reason brought to justify or understand its existence. I love you because—I just love you. This is not to say that there may not have been an initial reason, such as you are my child; I was struck by your physical presence; you are my sibling; I was captured by your way of being; we have spent many hours together. Any of these may have drawn us into contact, but my love for you can never be reduced to this, nor can it be explained by it.

In this way, to love someone is to accept her—as is.[39] That is not to say that I love all aspects of her, or that I don't wish or hope that part of her changes. But at the deepest level, to accept someone is to accept someone in their entirety, in their wholeness, absent any condition: as is. Love can be violated; it can be overcome; it can fade; but so long as it exists, it is unconditional. I love you just because of who you are and how you are, despite—and with!—those aspects of how you are that I do not love. To be sure, love entails more than this: from this starting point ensues a praxis of respect and responsibility.[40] Yet the essence of love—what envelopes and distinguishes the ensuing acts of respect and responsibility—is the initial posturing of unfettered acceptance.

So, too, does Divine love express itself toward the human being. I may struggle with this statement philosophically or theologically, demanding that the totally Other avoid any semblance of action that bears comparison to what we know from our humanity. But I cannot deny the reality of the occurrence, a foundational and ongoing event from which my deepest orientation in the world emerges. Only this philosophically- and theologically-problematic statement can launch a life of service. And only this absurd statement can resolve the absurdity of a human being "worthy" of Divine love, or the absurdity of the very possibility of the Divine loving a human being. It is neither difficult nor absurd for the Divine to love a creature—including a flawed one, such as me—because that is exactly what it means to love: to accept a creature *in toto*.

Have I not fallen captive to a feel-good theology that assures me: the Divine loves me as I am, and thus, comforted and nourished by that love, I find reason and justification to stay exactly as I am? The Torah would have it otherwise: to be loved is to be responsive to the lover. Love constitutes a kind of underbelly of the life of command, delicately touching areas of intimacy that *yir'a* cannot reach. Love, though it caresses, also commands: I am loved, and I wish to be worthy of that love, though I know with clarity and surety that I am not—yet. I am loved, and that nourishment provides me the sustenance of will to effectuate change. I am loved, and so I respond with attention and attentiveness to my lover. I am loved, and, having received a gift, I must share. Overwhelmed, the beloved must take her love out into the streets.

I am a child, taking my first steps, stumbling and falling—and I lift my eyes to see the joyful, loving glance of a parent, arms outstretched, eyes glimmering with excitement and love. I have not yet mastered the walking, but the loving glance enjoins me to arise anew and find the resolve and the ability to commit myself to moving forward.

To be loved by the Divine is to know that I am not yet there, but to experience the chasm that separates me from where I can and should be as a promise of growth rather than a condemnation of my present abilities—and inabilities. The light of the Divine countenance floods this gaping chasm, but, while highlighting the distance of separation, it illuminates a path, one among multiple paths, between which I must choose. The light, though strong, is too diffuse to illuminate just one path: yet its shining radiates warm embers that draw me near, enticing me to refuse the non-path of stillness, opting instead for a path of movement. The Divine, by addressing me and, in so doing, determining me as worthy of address, loves me, and this love commands.

And yet, even if we have resolved the plausibility of my being worthy of love of the Divine by touching upon that essential aspect of love as acceptance, we have spoken only of the possibility of the Divine loving me. The reality of Divine love holds within it a deeper secret, hinted by its incommensurability with human love. The strength of the grip of human love is directly proportional to its exclusivity. The deepest impulse behind monogamy is the sense that love—for the sake of its fullness and its ability to expand endlessly and inhabit every crevice that separates my lover from me—must be exclusive. Your total acceptance of me requires that the love itself be all-encompassing, which is to say, whole. Your acceptance of my partiality and incompleteness must, for the sake of its authenticity and effectiveness, be complete. This wholeness and completeness know neither bounds nor divisions, and that is the very meaning of its exclusivity. The love of lovers approximates this truth.

The love that transpires between parents and children is otherwise, but the child, by definition, cannot fathom this possibility. Siblings rival over parents' love because they cannot fathom that their parents can love a love other than the lover's love. Any impingement upon the exclusivity of the love sullies the love, marking it as partial, and, as such, incomplete and flawed. The child "knows" this even before she has tasted the love of the lover: from within the love emerges the demand of exclusivity. The demand to be loved is infinite; the ability to love, finite.

Levinas understood that the moment when two infinite demands clash in a world of finitude, a discipline of responsibility must be developed.[41] Neither the child nor the lover wants to know of a praxis of love. The beloved's demand for an infinite love can be negotiated: the lover bestows her love only upon the beloved. And while the finite realities of time and place set bounds to the love, no other beloved infringes upon the one and only beloved. And so a drop of infinity is preserved in the love.

It is otherwise with the beloved child. For her, not only do time and space curtail the love of the parent; so does the advent of another child. The sibling bursts into the beloved child's world with brutal elemental force; her very existence curtails the possibility of an infinite love.

Only the parent knows better. The parent knows that her love for each child is, to be sure, distinct, though no less complete for being so. Each love could not be more complete or more exact, and the existence of another sibling simply adds more love, different love; parental love cannot be diminished or extinguished. One child challenges, another is easy; one child fills the parent with angst, the other child serves as a source of pride: the parent loves each child differently, but each love is complete, and the loves are truly incomparable. The parent knows this, but only for her parental love and in her parental love; as a child—every parent, of course, is also a child—she is given to the throes of jealousy that her parents' love for her is made incomplete by her sibling.

Vis-à-vis the Divine, we are children; how could it be otherwise? Even if we have the higher parental understanding of the possibility of parental love, we nonetheless demand the love of the lover, exclusive as it is. Our encounter with the Divine, our receiving of the love of the Divine is that aloneness-together, that loneliness of two that Rosenzweig describes.[42] We know that we are not the only ones to have experienced the Divine—not in general, and not (even) right now. But we cannot imagine—and we most certainly cannot "make sense" of, or make peace with—the possibility that our lover, at the very moment of our intimacy, was whispering loving commands in the ear of someone else. But others make the claim, insisting that the Divine offered them love, and so we have to verify what we have heard. The commanding love I just experienced must be authenticated; it must enter the open expanse of intersubjective territory—for the sake of its authenticity, for the sake of its veracity.

The mystic, like the hermit, wants to stay in the cave; the allure of having the Divine all to myself is powerful, and the possibility of exiting into the bright light of day, into the field of human interaction and verification, only to discover that I misheard the words of the Divine, or that I heard them correctly but misunderstood them, or that I am not the only one upon whom the Divine bestowed a loving command is terrifying. It threatens to negate the love.

The command of the Divine is born of our moment of intimacy, but the unavoidable demand of the halakha is to bring the intimate commandment of Divine love into the daylight of its glance. To live halakhically is to respond to that love, to instantiate it in discrete action. To live halakhically is therefore to risk embarrassment, exposure, and error with each and every deed.

Ultimately, the halakha—to be true to itself and to its method, which is to say, to be true to the Divine—must itself stride into full daylight. For the halakha is merely one of the bodies that refracts light; it is not the source itself. The light of all being whispers commands lovingly to the individual and to the community, and each individual and community must be willing to stake its being on how to exit that moment of intimacy, and to face those who heard otherwise and who do differently. The most delicate moment of Shabbat is the moment of havdallah, that precipitous but invigorating transition to the work week. And there is work to be done.

## NOTES

1. See *Pesikta deRav Kahana* 12 [Hebrew].
2. Psalms 65:2.
3. Maimonides argues that "It is ... impossible that [God] should have affirmative attributes" (Maimonides, *Guide*, Volume 1, 135, corresponding to Part I Chapter 58). Addressing the person seeking to understand the Divine, he writes: "[I]n every case in which the demonstration that a certain thing

should be negated in reference to Him becomes clear to you, you become more perfect, and that in every case in which you affirm of Him an additional thing, you become one who likens him to other things and you get further away from the knowledge of His true reality" (Ibid., 139, corresponding to Part I Chapter 59).

4. Rosenzweig in *Franz Rosenzweig: His Life and Thought*, 243.
5. Gabriel Marcel, *Creative Fidelity*, translated by Robert Rosthal (New York: Cross Publishing, 1982), 36.
6. Rosenzweig, *The Star of Redemption*, 186–188.
7. Ibid., 167, 190, 201–202.
8. "And YHVH God created all of the beasts of the field and all of the fowl of the heavens out of the earth, and brought them to Adam to see what Adam would call them; and whatever Adam called that living creature – that was its name. And Adam issued names to each cattle and to the fowl of the heavens and to all of the beasts of the field; but there was nowhere to be found a helper to challenge Adam" (Genesis 2: 19–20). See also *Genesis Rabba* 17:4.
9. B.T. Bava Mezia 59b.
10. See Mishna Yoma 6:2; see also Ari Elon, *Yah BiShevat* (Bina: Tel Aviv, 1999) [Hebrew], 7–9.
11. Mishna Brakhot 2:8.
12. B.T. Brakhot 33b.
13. Levinas, *Totality and Infinity*, 48–52.
14. Rabbi Naḥman of Breslau, *Likkutei Moharan*, Part II, 48.
15. Barukh HaLevy Epstein, *Barukh She'Amar*, Tefillot Hashanah, 277–278 [Hebrew].
16. *Zohar*, Parashat Teruma, 135a–135b.
17. Isaiah 6:3. It is also part of the Shabbat morning liturgy: "And one called unto another and said: Holy, holy, holy is the God of hosts; the whole earth is fully of His glory."
18. II Samuel 7:23. It is also part of the Shabbat afternoon liturgy: "You are one and your name is one, and who is like your people Israel, one nation on this earth."
19. *Pesikta deRav Kahana* 12:6.
20. B.T. Megillah 13a: "Rabbi Yoḥanan said ... [that] anyone who repudiates idolatry is called *Yehudi* (a Jew)." See also Maimonides, *Mishneh Torah*, Laws of Idolatry, especially Chapter Two; Yeshayuhu Leibowitz, *Judaism, Human Values, and the Jewish State*, 86–87; and the excellent study of Moshe Halbertal and Avishai Margalit, *Idolatry* (Cambridge: Harvard University Press, 1992).
21. The charge to engage in works of social justice often finds its conceptual root in the idea of תיקון עולם [*tikkun olam*], which appears as a meta-halakhic principle in Mishna Gittin Chapter Four. See also B.T. Gittin, 32a ff.

22. Rooted in the Biblical verses which indicate that the Divine created the human being in the image of the Divine (Genesis 1: 26–27), the idea that the human being contains infinite worth develops a kind of independence from its theological origin. See also Mishna Sanhedrin 4:5 and Yair Lorberbaum's acclaimed study *In God's Image: Myth, Theology* (New York: Cambridge University Press, 2015).

23. "Rabbi Huna and Rabbi Jeremiah said in the name of Rabbi Ḥiyya b. Abba: It is written, *They have forsaken Me and have not kept My law* (Jeremiah 16:2) – i.e., Would that they had forsaken Me but kept My law, since by occupying themselves therewith, the light which it contains would have led them back to the right path." *Midrash Rabbah: Lamentations,* trans. A Cohen, ed. H. Freedman (New York: Soncino, 1983), 2–3.

24. Rabbi Simḥa Bunam of Peshischa, *Kol Simḥa,* Parashat VaYetze.

25. Yeshayahu Leibowitz, *Judaism, Human Values, and the Jewish State,* 28.

26. David Hartman, *A Heart of Many Rooms: Celebrating the Many Voices within Judaism* (Woodstock, Vermont: Jewish Lights, 1999), xxiii.

27. Emmanuel Levinas, *Difficult Freedom* (Baltimore, Johns Hopkins University Press, 1990), 6.

28. Zohar, Parashat Terumah, 135a–135b.

29. Zekharia 14:9.

30. Mishna Shabbat 1:1.

31. B.T. Shabbat 118–119.

32. B.T. Shabbat 88a.

33. B.T. Brakhot 33b.

34. "Rabba bar Rav Huna said: Any person who has Torah in him but does not have fear of Heaven is like a treasurer to whom they gave keys to the inner doors of the treasury but they did not give keys to the outer door. With what key will he enter?" (B.T. Shabbat 31b).

35. Hartman, *The God Who Hates Lies,* 37.

36. *Sifrei Devarim,* Parashat Va'Etḥanan 32.

37. Jerusalem Talmud, Sotah 5.

38. B.T. Kiddushin 39b.

39. It is not insignificant that the Hebrew word for acceptance is קבלה, the same term used for the Jewish mystical tradition.

40. Erich Fromm, *The Art of Loving* (New York: Harper, 2006), 26, Buber, *I and Thou,* trans. Walter Kaufman (New York: Charles Scribner's Sons, 1970), 66.

41. Emmanuel Levinas, *Totality and Infinity,* 212 ff.

42. *Franz Rosenzweig: His Life and Thought,* 243.

# EPILOGUE

## PARTING WAYS

Just before we part ways, we take an accounting of the path we shared, of our shared time. In the pages that follow, I part ways from the reader.

Deuteronomy 22:1-4 enjoins us to return a lost object to its rightful owner.[1] In an astoundingly attentive reading of those verses, the rabbis codify that we have two options if we chance upon a lost object.[2] Either that object is now legally mine because circumstances forced the (former) owner to forfeit any chance of claiming it, or it still rightfully belongs to the former owner, in which case I am now obligated to find that owner and return the lost property. The key word in those Biblical verses—"you may not ignore [the object]"—achieves legal instantiation: if the owner still has a claim on the object, I may not carry on my way and pass it by; I must assume responsibility for the object and do my utmost to return that object to its owner, even if doing so requires hardship. On the basis of a sensitive reading of the Biblical injunction "you may not ignore [the object]," the rabbis not only translate into clear, legal terms the moral quandary as to what we must do if happening upon a lost object. They do so while expressing a keen awareness of the deep human inclination to ignore the object, and an uncompromising commitment to the religious demand of the hour—namely, to resist that temptation and to reveal that there lurks a person behind this object, someone who has lost an object and to whom I have an obligation. The rabbis' reading is masterful because they have combined remarkable attentiveness to the Biblical text with insightful religious

L. Wiener Dow, *The Going*,
https://doi.org/10.1007/978-3-319-68831-2

sensibility, uniting those two forces into a pragmatic of practice that gives precise, if demanding, expression to both commitments.

In crafting the halakha as a whole, the rabbis offer a similarly masterful reading of the Torah's most basic injunction and overarching command- ment: to testify to the presence of the Divine through our actions by living a commanded life of holiness. Holiness is the path I travel; it is not a destina- tion. From the first commandment to the first Jew, when the Divine enjoins Abraham לֶךְ לְךָ [*Lekh lekha*]: Go forth, get going!; to the seminal commandment issued to all of Israel to bind the words of Torah upon ourselves and speak them constantly as we walk upon our way: וּבְלֶכְתְּךָ בַדֶּרֶךְ [ *U-velekhtekha va-derekh*]; up until the final verse of the Torah, which ends with the people beholding the Land of Israel, but not yet having entered: we are a people on the way. In fact, even when we will arrive in the Land of Israel, the Torah obligates us to remain strangers and temporary residents (Leviticus 25:23): we are destined to seek, duty-bound not to arrive. Neither the Torah nor rabbinic literature offers us a home: this fused Written-Oral Torah commands us a way. The rabbis knew with paramount sensitivity and wisdom how to craft the Torah's inchoate command into a complex nexus of religious commitment.

In order to get at my understanding of how the halakha that left the workshop of the rabbinic artisans achieves just that, I needed to start at the beginning, with my beginnings, as I do in Chap. 1. "Beginnings" expresses a dual commitment: on the one hand, what it means to philosophize; on the other, how we engage—and are engaged by—the halakha.

Franz Rosenzweig aptly understands philosophical knowledge to emerge from a glance at something past. But I would add that the "point of view" philosopher[3] whom he praises must, for the sake of the experience-based philosophy that he espouses, begin with an accounting of his own experi- ences—the ones upon the basis of which he has begun his process of reflection. So there I must start. My musings on time, language, commu- nity, and the Divine are borne of, and inseparable from, the wealth of my experiences. My understanding and experience of the halakha are largely much functions of the Jewish way I have traveled, even as they are also a reflection of that way.

But this starting point results not only from my philosophical commit- ments; it is bound together intimately with my understanding of the halakha as the rabbis fashioned it. To live a life of halakha is to listen, to be on the way, to experiment, to place oneself on a precarious perch between the received tradition and the reality into which we are thrust by some combination of circumstance and choice. The king must write his own *sefer Torah*,[4] and each of us must write her own book on halakha, a book whose covers are our birth and our death, and the lines we scribble, the moments of lived life. Rava understood that I cannot experience the halakha other than from my own vantage point: The judge has only what his eyes can see, he says.[5]

In this sense, this book is not only an expression of my understanding of halakha; it is an act of testimony. The meditation as a whole constitutes an attempt to do to the halakha what, as I write in Chaps. 3 and 4, the halakha itself endeavors to do: namely, to drag the intimate experience of and with the Divine into the harsh daylight of verification and shared discourse. In it, I testify to (part of) my experience of the Divine, and to my experience of the ways in which the halakha as a way of life consists of translating the private language of the intimate encounter with the Divine into a public praxis of action that, as such, enters into the realm of shared communal discourse. Exposing such an experience is a risk, but keeping it private— while securer—is sacrilege. עת לעשות לה' הפרו תורתך [*Eit la'asot la-Shem, heifeiro toratekha*] (Psalms 119:126). "The time has come to act for the Divine": violating the perfect silence of truth reflects a commitment to the command to engage in Torah. The sages understood that lived life is both an expression of halakha and a source of Torah.[6] That is what this meditation aims to be.

Perhaps the single greatest truth that the halakha offers—and that which I tried to articulate in Chap. 2: "Saying, Writing, Doing"—is that we cannot speak *about* the Divine; we respond to the Divine through action. The Torah can and must talk, and this talking orients us and our doing. But the halakha *does*, and when it comes to theology, doing manages to articulate that which refuses to be bound by language. And yet, just as the glance articulates something that is beyond language while nonetheless being predicated on it,[7] the halakha requires a language beyond which it can stride, and on the basis of which it can express that which is inexpressible. The Torah is that language, and the rabbis fashioned a sense of Torah that allows the voice of the Divine constantly to break forth out of the shackles of the word into the living present. The delicate weave that they establish between the Written and the Oral Torahs is what allows them—and the historical community of Israel—to negotiate between eternity*qua* immutability and eternity*qua* the constancy of a Divine voice that beckons us here, now.

The Divine voice that bursts forth into the wide open from the written verses of Torah demands actualization, and the halakha is its fulfillment. The unremitting insistence of the halakha is that the encounter with the Divine must, for the sake of its veracity, find expression in the world. Like the love of *The Song of Songs* that must be declared in the streets, the intimacy of the aloneness-together with the Divine resists being confined in the inner chambers. The intensity of the encounter contains a double-charge: the centrifugal force turns centripetal, and the outward effect spreads into the world. Holiness must manifest itself in all aspects of life, private and public. The "language" of doing thus becomes constitutive of community: the halakha, in this respect, is none other than the shared doing of the Jewish community.

In Chap. 3: "Shared Spacetime," I spell out the way in which the halakha, through some of its central operating categories, negotiates this fruitful tension between the intimacy of the aloneness-together of individual experience and the fundamental command that this intimacy receive expression in the shared space of the community. Not only is this tension between the individual and the community never resolved; it in fact expands outwardly and becomes manifest disagreement, *mahloket*—initially between different individuals who understand the dictates of the Divine in conflicting ways. This disagreement, in turn, continues its course, as differing communities live out different understandings of the halakha. The "and" of the halakha becomes a theological tenet, as disparate and cacophonous aspects of reality congeal to form a conglomerate that expresses and testifies to the oneness of the Divine.

And so it was that in the next and final Chap. 4, "The Ineffable," I needed to go against the grain of that single greatest truth that the halakha offers, and I attempt to articulate that which the halakha knows to be beyond articulation. For there is no halakha without that Nameless One, and any effort to spell out what the halakha is about that fails to confront this insurmountable challenge will surely fail in capturing that wondrous force that generates the pulse of halakhic movement. The halakha rests upon a theology of command, and it is that to which I try to give a moment in Chap. 4. Perhaps Chap. 4 is less a theology of command than it is a phenomenology of command—because, after all, what I can say about the Divine is quite limited.

Once the halakha is properly contextualized as a path to the Divine, the "and" of the halakha becomes a mere premonition to the great "and" of any theological effort. The Divine is more than my, or my community's, experience with/of it. Moreover, even within my innermost experience of the Divine, voices resound that do not have overtones of command such as those that I articulate in Chap. 4. But alas, I have not tried to say it all: only to hold on tenuously to one of the undertones of the Divine, just long enough to bring a microphone in its proximity in a futile effort to allow its voice to be amplified beyond the confines of intimate encounter. A fuller theology—for me, but also for the Torah and for Judaism—requires an attentiveness to other theological moments, containing overtones and undertones of striking variety, especially of a feminist tenor.

This work, then, points beyond itself. But before parting ways by pointing to what this work is not, it is important to say what I hope it may still be.

First and foremost, I hope that *The Going* has fashioned a portrait of the halakha and a narrative of what it means to live a life informed by and committed to the halakha, one that is recognizable to those who place themselves within its dictates. And yet, I hope that the portrait that I have sketched offers even to those intimately familiar with the halakha from within the possibility of an experience of discovery in the way that reflective consideration of that which is most familiar can often surprise us with unanticipated revelation. Accompanying a tourist in our homeland can awaken us to elements that are so familiar to us that we fail to see or appreciate them, and I hope that I have offered herein such a journey— one that allows the halakhically-lived life to achieve a moment of clarity, intelligibility, and coherence for its adherent.

I also hope that *The Going* has offered a journey deep into the heartland of halakha for those who live elsewhere, beyond its borders. The halakha, of course, is a lived life, and so no visitor confined to a tourist bus traveling along its roads can truly understand what it is to step out of the bus, travel off the road, or change one's status from tourist to citizen. (Remarkably, the halakha offers just that possibility—that membership in the Jewish collective has a normative gate through which one can pass and attain full-fledged citizenship, but alas—that is for a different conversation, and neither I nor the halakha has any stake in encouraging tourists to change their status and stay.) I am exceedingly happy to have tourists come and visit, for—as we saw in Chap. 3—one of the deepest impulses in the Torah is that it, and the halakhic lifestyle that emerges from its commanding voice, must be intelligible to those who are not devoted to its dictates. כי היא חכמתכם ובינתכם לעיני העמים [*ki hi ḥokhmatkhem u-vinatkhem be-einei ha-amim*]. For they are your wisdom and your understanding in the eyes of the nations.[8]

I also harbor two final hopes for this work.

If, at some level, my words allow any reader to elevate even one of her actions and release a spark of holiness in this world, then I will have succeeded in augmenting the presence of the Divine in the world. Testimony is not ultimately about stating the truth; it is informed and motivated by the desire to allow that truth to reverberate and fill the world with the beauty of its sound.

As my efforts on this work were drawing to a close, I had the blessing of being asked by one of my teenage daughters questions about belief and a life committed to halakha. I tried to answer the best I could, without referring her to "Chapter This" or "page that," but I did have a sense of clarity that beyond offering my children my lived life, I might also be obligated to offer them an articulate Torah that elucidates those beliefs and understandings that inform my observance of halakha. Three times daily, we declare that an integral part of our going on the way is teaching Torah to our children, those whom we trust to establish with sensitivity and with fortitude a path, their path, the path of the *halakha*.

## Notes

1. "You shall not see your brother's ox or sheep straying away and ignore them; rather, you shall take them back to your brother. If your brother does not reside near you or you do not know who he is, you shall bring it to your own house, and it shall remain with you until your brother claims it; then you shall return it. And so shall you do the same with his donkey; and so shall you do with his garment; and so shall you do with anything that your brother loses and you find. You cannot ignore it. You shall not see your brother's donkey or ox fallen on the road and ignore them; you shall help him lift it up" (Deuteronomy 22:1–4).
2. Mishna Bava Meẓia 2:1–2.
3. Franz Rosenzweig, *The Star of Redemption*, 6–9, 105–106.
4. Deuteronomy 17:18.
5. B.T. Bava Batra 131a.
6. Ben-Menahem, "Two Talmudic Understandings."
7. Martin Buber, *I and Thou*, 56–57.
8. See Chap. 3 note 35.

# INDEX

Note: Page number followed by 'n' refers to notes

© The Author(s) 2017
L. Wiener Dow, *The Going*,
https://doi.org/10.1007/978-3-319-68831-2

CPSIA information can be obtained
at www.ICGtesting.com
Printed in the USA
LVOW13*1120210218

567395LV00009B/31/P